SO-BZP-000

The U.S. Naval Institute on

THE UNITED STATES
COAST GUARD

U.S. NAVAL INSTITUTE
Chronicles

For nearly a century and a half since a group
of concerned naval officers gathered to provide
a forum for the exchange of constructive ideas,
the U.S. Naval Institute has been a unique
source of information relevant to the nation's
sea services. Through the open forum provided
by *Proceedings* and *Naval History* magazines,
Naval Institute Press (the book-publishing arm
of the institute), a robust Oral History program,
and more recent immersion in various cyber
activities (including the *Naval Institute Blog*
and *Naval Institute News*), USNI has built a
vast assemblage of intellectual content that has
long supported the Navy, Marine Corps, and
Coast Guard as well as the nation as a whole.

Recognizing the potential value of this
exceptional collection, USNI has embarked
on a number of new platforms to reintroduce
readers to significant portions of this virtual
treasure trove. The U.S. Naval Institute
Chronicles series focuses on the relevance of
history by resurrecting appropriate selections
that are built around various themes, such as
battles, personalities, and service components.
Available in both paper and eBook versions,
these carefully selected volumes help readers
navigate through this intellectual labyrinth by
providing some of the best contributions that
have provided unique perspectives and helped
shape naval thinking over the many decades
since the institute's founding in 1873.

The U.S. Naval Institute on

THE UNITED STATES COAST GUARD

THOMAS J. CUTLER
Series Editor

Naval Institute Press
Annapolis, Maryland

Naval Institute Press
291 Wood Road
Annapolis, MD 21402

© 2017 by the U.S. Naval Institute
All rights reserved. No part of this book may be reproduced or utilized in any
form or by any means, electronic or mechanical, including photocopying and
recording, or by any information storage and retrieval system, without permission
in writing from the publisher.

Library of Congress Cataloging-in-Publication Data
Names: Cutler, Thomas J., date, editor of compilation. | United States Naval
    Institute, issuing body.
Title: The U.S. Naval Institute on the United States Coast Guard / Thomas J. Cutler.
Description: Annapolis, Maryland : Naval Institute Press, [2017] | Series:
    U.S. Naval Institute chronicles | Includes bibliographical references and index.
Identifiers: LCCN 2016031364 (print) | LCCN 2016035111 (ebook) |
    ISBN 9781682470466 (pbk. : alk. paper) | ISBN 9781682470473 (ePub) |
    ISBN 9781682470473 (ePDF) | ISBN 9781682470473 (mobi)
Subjects: LCSH: United States. Coast Guard. | United States. Coast Guard—History.
Classification: LCC VG53 .U58 2017 (print) | LCC VG53 (ebook) |
    DDC 363.28/60973—dc23
LC record available at https://lccn.loc.gov/2016031364

♾ Print editions meet the requirements of ANSI/NISO z39.48–1992
(Permanence of Paper).
Printed in the United States of America.

25 24 23 22 21 20 19 18 17   9 8 7 6 5 4 3 2 1
First printing

CONTENTS

EDITOR'S NOTE

BECAUSE THIS BOOK is an anthology, containing documents from different time periods, the selections included here are subject to varying styles and conventions. Other variables are introduced by the evolving nature of the Naval Institute's publication practices. For those reasons, certain editorial decisions were required in order to avoid introducing confusion or inconsistencies and to expedite the process of assembling these sometimes disparate pieces.

Gender

Most jarring of the differences that readers will encounter are likely those associated with gender. A number of the included selections were written when the armed forces were primarily a male domain and so adhere to purely masculine references. I have chosen to leave the original language intact in these documents for the sake of authenticity and to avoid the complications that can arise when trying to make anachronistic adjustments. So readers are asked to "translate" (converting the ubiquitous "he" to "he or she" and "his" to "her or his" as required) and, while doing so, to celebrate the progress that we have made in these matters in more recent times.

Author "Biographies"

Another problem arises when considering biographical information of the various authors whose works make up this special collection. Some of the selections included in this anthology were originally accompanied by biographical information about their authors. Others were not. Those "biographies" that do exist have been included. They pertain to the time the article was written and may vary in terms of length and depth, some amounting to a single sentence pertaining to the author's current duty station, others consisting of several paragraphs that cover the author's career.

Ranks

I have retained the ranks of the authors *at the time of their publication.* As noted above, some of the authors wrote early in their careers, and the sagacity of their earlier contributions says much about the individuals, about the significance of the Naval Institute's forum, and about the importance of writing to the naval services—something that is sometimes underappreciated.

Other Anomalies

Readers may detect some inconsistencies in editorial style, reflecting staff changes at the Naval Institute, evolving practices in publishing itself, and various other factors not always identifiable. Some of the selections will include citational support, others will not. Authors sometimes coined their own words and occasionally violated traditional style conventions. *Bottom line:* with the exception of the removal of some extraneous materials (such as section numbers from book excerpts) and the conversion to a consistent font and overall design, these articles and excerpts appear as they originally did when first published.

ACKNOWLEDGMENTS

THIS PROJECT would not be possible without the dedication and remarkable industry of Denis Clift, the Naval Institute's vice president for planning and operations and president emeritus of the National Intelligence University. This former naval officer, who served in the administrations of eleven successive U.S. presidents and was once editor in chief of *Proceedings* magazine, bridged the gap between paper and electronics by single-handedly reviewing the massive body of the Naval Institute's intellectual content to find many of the treasures included in this anthology.

A great deal is also owed to Mary Ripley, Janis Jorgensen, Rebecca Smith, Judy Heise, Debbie Smith, Elaine Davy, and Heather Lancaster who devoted many hours and much talent to the digitization project that is at the heart of these anthologies.

Introduction

THE UNITED STATES COAST GUARD is a unique entity. Title 14 of the United States Code states: "The Coast Guard as established January 28, 1915, shall be a military service and a branch of the armed forces of the United States at all times." As members of a military service, Coast Guardsmen are subject to the Uniform Code of Military Justice and receive the same pay and allowances as members of the same pay grades in their four sister services. Yet the Coast Guard does not operate as an entity of the Department of Defense. In time of war, or when directed by the president, the Coast Guard can operate as a service within the Department of the Navy, but in peacetime it operates under the Department of Homeland Security, and the Commandant of the Coast Guard reports to the secretary of that cabinet department.

The history of this unusual service is also somewhat complicated. The Coast Guard celebrates its birthday as 4 August 1790 when Secretary of the Treasury Alexander Hamilton, the first to hold that office, created a system of cutters to enforce tariff and customs laws. But its origins can be traced further back to 1789, when the U.S. Lighthouse Service was established—although it did not officially become part of the Coast Guard until 1939, nearly twenty-five years after the Coast Guard had been officially established when the Life-Saving Service was combined with the Revenue Cutter Service.

As a component of America's sea services, the Coast Guard has frequently found its way into the pages of *Proceedings* magazine, and over the years the Naval Institute Press has published a number of Coast Guard–related books, including *The Coast Guardsman's Manual* beginning in 1952. These collected works could fill many volumes, but a few of the more interesting and relevant contributions are here gathered, beginning with the Quasi-War with France shortly after the nation's founding. Readers will discover or be reminded that the Coast Guard has played a role in a number of the nation's wars, including the war with Spain near the end of the nineteenth century, the Second World War—one of those times when the Coast Guard was a part of the Navy—and into the brown and green waters of Vietnam. Contributing authors include officers and enlisted, such as Claiborne Pell, who later became a well-known member of Congress, and Admiral Loy, who served as commandant from 1998 to 2002 and subsequently headed the Department of Homeland Security.

It is probably fair to say that the Coast Guard is largely underappreciated—often overshadowed by its big sister, the Navy, and more often than not forced to "make do" with limited resources—yet, as is evident in these pages, the nation would be hard-pressed to function without this diminutive but potent service. As is explained in the excerpt from Jim Dolbow's *The Coast Guardsman's Manual*, tenth edition, these specialized "sailors" tend the buoys that mark the nation's waterways, conduct maritime intercept operations, interdict drug traffic, enforce U.S. immigration laws at sea, police the nation's "Exclusive Economic Zone," conduct search and rescue operations when needed, provide ice-breaking services, and . . . The list goes on and on, making it abundantly clear that the nation is indeed fortunate to have such a service and making it also clear that this service should not be taken for granted. Through dedicated effort, frequent sacrifice, and an ethos that includes the words "protect," "defend," and "save," the men and women of the United States Coast Guard live up to their motto *Semper Paratus* (Always Prepared) every hour of every day.

1 "The Revenue Cutters in the Quasi-War with France"

Lieutenant (jg) R. W. Daly, USCGR

U.S. Naval Institute *Proceedings* (December 1942): 1713–23

IN 1798, THE UNITED STATES DRIFTED into an undeclared war with the Republic of France. The necessity to fight found us ill-prepared. Such naval vessels as we possessed were under the authority of the War Department, while their number and condition reflected the thrift rather than the vision of Congress. Troubles with the Barbary States had induced our legislators to provide a meager establishment of frigates and sloops to protect our commerce, but the seeming composition of our differences with Algiers had legally terminated the construction of these vessels. However, some ships, such as the *Constellation*, were near completion, and Navy-conscious statesmen were able to persuade their fellows that it would be the better part of economy to finish them. Thus, in the early days of our history, the Revenue Cutters of the Treasury Department composed a significant force.[1]

Established under Hamilton in 1790, the service had eight vessels of sufficient size to be considered capable of offensive operations, and these were transferred to the Navy for war duty, thus setting a precedent which was to be observed whenever the United States fought at sea. During the Quasi-War, the cutters comprised about 15 per cent of our armed maritime force, and captured at least 16 hostile vessels, out of the 92 taken, besides restoring many American ships to their owners.[2]

With isolated incidents abroad, the war was confined to the West Indies, where both parties were most vulnerable. Martinique was in British possession from 1793 until the Peace of Paris, 1802,[3] and Basse Terre Roads became the main base for the United States Fleet. The privateers out of Guadeloupe gave the most trouble, some 60 to 80 craft operating from that island.[4] Benjamin Stoddert, our first Secretary of the Navy, believed that depredations upon our commerce would cease if our ships could capture two or three thousand French seamen, and was, for that reason, opposed to wholesale exchange of prisoners.[5]

It was a cruising war. The Navy had orders to grant convoy to American merchantmen in the area, but not to employ their whole force for that purpose. In general, the merchantmen were to be convoyed clear of the West Indies, and then left to themselves, unless some naval vessel was returning to the United States, when convoy would be afforded for the remainder of the voyage.[6] Stoddert was emphatic that naval craft sail individually, writing to one commander,

> Although I have already said so much on the subject, I cannot conclude without again attempting to impress upon your mind the disadvantages of suffering our vessels to cruise in company. Cruising in Squadrons for small privateers seems of all means the best to avoid capturing them. It teaches the Commanders of the small vessels a reliance on force—not their own, for their protection. It is enough to make them Cowards. It prevents all means of knowing who are brave among them—because none are exposed to danger.[7]

And again, he said,

> Our whole Commerce can be best protected by employing our Public Armed Ships in cruising—especially the fast Sailors—while we are convoying in one place, we are attacked in another.[8]

We subscribed, therefore, to the French concept of a *guerre de course*, rather than to fleet action, which was, in view of our dismal equipment, denied us.

The United States and Great Britain more or less co-operated to meet this mutual threat to their trade, and American naval ships indiscriminately protected those of British or American registry. The Royal Navy and ours even had a system of private recognition signals, with adaptations to cover all conditions of meeting.[9]

In this war, the *Eagle* and the *Pickering* were very successful, and their records are worth investigating as representative of the best among the small American cruisers; the record of the *General Greene*, however, was perhaps more typical. The three together will give an insight into the manner in which the war was carried on.

It is to be remembered that these vessels lost their peace-time character as revenue cutters, being lost in the effort of the nation to create a Navy.

The *"Eagle"*

Built at Philadelphia in 1798, she was a 187-ton brig with a 58-foot keel, 20-foot beam, and a 9-foot hold, manned by a crew of 70. She was armed with fourteen 6-pounders, and was commanded by Hugh G. Campbell up to November, 1800, and by M. Simmones Bunbury from that date until the end of the war.[10]

The *Eagle* was a lucky ship, between March 2, 1799 and August 22, 1800, capturing five Frenchmen, retaking seven Americans, and assisting in the capturing or retaking of ten other French or American vessels.[11]

In August, 1798, the *Eagle* being ready to receive her guns, Captain Campbell was ordered to recruit men and store provisions, preparatory to joining Captain Murray of the *Montezuma*, 20, at Norfolk for a cruise to the West Indian station.[12] Dissatisfied with his equipment and delayed by a yellow-fever epidemic then in Philadelphia, Campbell attempted to comply with these instructions but was unable to do so, causing Stoddert to complain that he wanted energy.[13] On October 13, Stoddert very bluntly reprimanded Campbell for failure to make the rendezvous, and sent him alternate orders to protect the Georgia coast in event that Murray sailed before the *Eagle* reached Norfolk.[14] In a sense, it was perhaps fortunate for the Secretary of the Navy that Campbell's enforced delay prevented him from going at once to the West Indies, because in November, Stoddert found occasion to write consolingly to the worried Governor of Georgia, who was alarmed about the possibility of "piratical incursions" into his state, that

> Capt. Campbell in the Revenue Cutter *Eagle* of 14 guns, a well-armed vessel, has been ordered to make the Coasts of Georgia, the particular object of his protection.[15]

The protection did not last long, however, for the next month Campbell was ordered to quit Savannah and go down to Prince Rupert's Bay, where he would place himself under the direction of Captain John Barry of the 44-gun frigate *United States*.[16] En route, Campbell retook from a mutinous crew the schooner *Eliza*, out of Philadelphia bound for St. Thomas. Putting the mutineers in chains, Campbell transferred them to a homeward bound naval vessel; they were eventually convicted and hanged.[17] Before reporting to Barry, he also rescued the sloop *Lark* from her French prize crew.[18] Early in the evening of March 14, he fell in with the American Squadron, among which was the *Pickering*, a cutter identical to the *Eagle* except in armament, and accompanied them to Prince Rupert's Bay.[19]

After a week, Campbell left the bay for a cruise in company with the *United States*, *Constitution*, 44, Captain Samuel Nicholson, and *Merrimac*, 24, Captain Moses Brown.[20] Within a few days, Campbell had recaptured another sloop, and on April 5, after a chase, made a prize of the sloop *Bonpere*. This privateer was manned by 52 men, mostly negroes, and armed with six guns, all but two 4-pounders being thrown overboard during the pursuit. The sloop was ultimately sold in Georgia to the government for a trifle more than $2,000, and converted into a revenue cutter assigned to that state.[21]

By the middle of the month, Campbell had returned to the bay and been sent with Nicholson to see a fleet of 33 merchantmen safely out of the danger zone. He was primarily occupied in chasing any stranger who might have hostile intentions, but apparently encountered no trouble.[22] Early in May, in the new squadron rendezvous of Basse Terre Road, Campbell was assigned with Lieutenant Speake of the *Richmond*, 18, to patrol to windward of Barbuda and Antigua. This duty was highlighted by May 15, when Speake and Campbell retook the ship *Nancy* and the brig *Mahitable*.[23]

May 20, 1799, the Navy Department incorporated the *Pickering*, *Scammel*, and *Eagle* in the regular establishment, and returned the *Diligence* and *General Greene* to the Treasury Department. Strictly speaking, of course, the subsequent activities of the *Eagle* were naval, but the ship, crew, and officers were of the Revenue Cutter Service.[24] Late in July, Campbell was commissioned a Master Commandant in the Navy.[25]

May 29, in company with the *Baltimore*, 20, Captain Samuel Barron, the *Eagle* took the *Siren*, of 4 guns and 36 men, in the words of Captain Thomas Tingey, then commanding the squadron, "a very small French privateer."[26] On the same day, falling in with the *United States*, the *Eagle* assisted in retaking the sloop *Hudson*.[27]

In mid-June, the *Eagle* and *Richmond* left St. Kitts with another convoy, which they escorted as far as the Bermudas before slanting off for Hampton Roads, where they stayed a short time before returning to Basse Terre by the 25th.[28] A delay in the receipt of orders mistakenly sent them back to Norfolk. They arrived on July 2, and Stoddert directed them to prepare for immediate return.[29] Campbell, however, needed officers, and asked for them. The Secretary of the Navy, possibly influenced by Campbell's record as a light ship commander, had changed his opinion of him, and wrote a very cordial reply, concluding, in a form close to apology, "I fix on the 25th Inst for your sailing but if you sail sooner it will be a new proof that I did you an injustice last year in supposing you might have got sooner to sea. . . ."[30] Campbell's preparations were interrupted on the 18th by a hurried request from Stoddert to hunt for a French privateer of 16 guns which was reported to have stopped an American schooner off Little Egg Harbor. The alarm was without foundation,[31] and may have been one of the causes for Campbell's failure to give the Secretary the "new proof" desired. Be that as it may, Campbell was sent his orders on August 8 to depart for Guadeloupe within twelve hours. He carried dispatches for Tingey.[32]

He was returning none too soon to the station. Harassed, Tingey was pleading with Stoddert to send him experienced officers like "Barron, Bainbridge and Campbell."[33]

Early in September, the *Eagle* was with the *Delaware*, 20, Captain Thomas Baker, when the French sloop *Reynold* passed into American hands.[34] At this time, the privateers were also using Puerto Rico, but the greatest number continued to come from Guadeloupe. Tingey had done his part to win the war, and Captain Richard Morris was instructed to ready the *Adams*, 28, and take command.[35]

September 19, Campbell recaptured the American brig *North Carolina*, and October 2 he was in company with Tingey's *Ganges* when the French schooner *Esperance* struck her colors.[36] A midshipman, John Kiddall, summarized the cruise of the *Eagle* up to November 20:

> The first island we put into after leaving the *Delaware* was St. Kitts. Shortly after we cruized to windward and have had the good fortune of retaking one American brig, which was in tow of a French Schooner privateer, which we drove ashore, but after beating some time, got off and run for cover of a Fort. We have likewise taken two French vessels, one a sloop laden with sugar and molasses, the other a Letter of Marque laden with sugar and coffee, bound to France. . . . When we captured the last mentioned the *Ganges* was in company with us . . . the American brig I brought into St. Kitts. We are now bound out as convoy for some American vessels.[37]

Under the prize system of the old Navy, Campbell began to make a small fortune. December 5 he retook the brig *George* and on January 2, 1800, the brig *Polly*. The 10th of that month, the *Adams* and the *Eagle* captured the French schooner *Fougueuse* of 70 men and 2 guns, as well as recovering the American schooner *Aphia*.[38] These brought the total captures of Morris's command to 17 ships.[39] February 1, alone, the *Eagle* took the schooner *Benevolence*,[40] and a few days later was seriously mauled. "The brig *Eagle* . . . chaced two French privateers, but finding their force double his own, did not think prudent to engage, but continued his course; after receiving a number of shot from them."[41] On March 1, Campbell seized the American schooner *Three Friends*, and on April 1, overpowered the French schooner *Favorite*.[42]

By May, although seriously in need of sails, the *Eagle* picked up the tiny schooner *La Magdelaine* of 15 tons and 4 men.[43] On the 7th, the prize crew aboard the American sloop *Ann*, Master Reuben Barnes, surrendered to the cutter's guns, as did the Frenchmen aboard the schooner *Hope*, three days later.[44] Towards the latter part of June, Campbell had a brush with a privateer off St. Bartholomews, which had three prizes, two English brigs and a Yankee sloop, in company. The privateer managed to escape after cutting the *Eagle*'s sails and rigging to pieces, but Campbell had the doubtful consolation of forcing the prize crews to run their vessels aground.[45]

The cruise continued to be profitable. On June 25, Campbell, damages repaired, captured the French schooner *Dolphin*, and on August 22 another schooner, *La Tourterelle*.[46] This was the last of his triumphs. His battered ship urgently needed refitting in the States. "The *Eagle* will want Coppering, her bottom being in a Miserable Condition, half her Copper being off."[47] So, homeward bound by September 3, he was in the harbor of St. Thomas, together with Captain John Rodgers of the *Maryland*, 20, and a gathering convoy of 52 Americans, waiting for a hurricane to cease. The southerly gales slacked off after a week and the ships sailed.[48]

September 28, Campbell arrived at Newcastle, where the *Eagle* was to be overhauled for another hitch in the Indies.[49] For his valuable services, Campbell was promoted to the command of the 28-gun frigate *General Greene* in November, and, ultimately, Lieutenant M. Simmones Bunbury was assigned the *Eagle*.[50] The difficulty with the French was nearing its solution, and Bunbury's instructions were less militant than those which had originally been given Campbell in the years previous. Speaking of the operations of French privateers, Stoddert directed Bunbury that,

> If they continue, you must capture in your turn; but if they cease to molest our vessels, you will so conduct yourself, as to evince the sincerity of our pacific dispositions towards them.[51]

Bunbury didn't have a chance for glory. His cruise in the Indies was without notable event. While the *Eagle* was at sea, Stoddert secured Congressional passage of the Peace Establishment Act, which created a permanent list of ships and officers. Campbell was retained as a Captain, but his old ship was not.[52] Arriving at Baltimore in June, 1801, she was sold for $10,600.[53]

The "*General Greene*"

A 98-ton sloop built at Philadelphia in 1797, she had a far less spectacular career than the *Eagle*. With a crew of 34 men to handle her ten 4-pounders, she joined the Navy in the summer of 1798.[54] On July 14, Captain George Price, U.S.R.C.S., reported that he would be ready for sea as soon as he had obtained a full complement.[55] A few days later, he received orders to cruise between Cape Henry and Long Island in company with the *Ganges*, 24, Captain Richard Dale, and the cutter *Governor Jay*, 14, Captain John W. Leonard, U.S.R.C.S., the ships to be under Dale's command.[56]

By the end of the month, Price was on the station, cruising alone, inasmuch as neither ship had joined him. In the meantime, the *Baltimore*,

20, Captain Isaac Phillips, had instructions to replace the *Ganges*, which was to go on convoy duty to the West Indies with Captain Thomas Truxtun, never having reached the station to which she had been first ordered. In the interim, Captain Nicholson and the *Constitution* were to assume the responsibility.[57] The cutters, however, apparently had full responsibility for the protection of the coast. In that day of clumsy communications, it is interesting to note that Price had instructions to appear about every ten or twelve days off Cape Henlopen, flying the Swedish flag; after a day or two, he could expect messages from Philadelphia.[58] Another cutter, the *Virginia*, 14, Captain Francis Bright, covered the waters from Cape Henry south to Florida. In August, Nicholson's little flotilla was transferred to this territory.[59]

After this cruising, the *General Greene* put into Chester for refitting, and in October got new sailing orders.[60] Reinforced by ten marines in addition to her crew, she was sent to New York to rendezvous with the *Governor Jay*. The cutters were to escort the supply ship *America* to the West Indies,[61] the *America* being burdened with 10 tons of ship bread, and 100 barrels each of beef and pork. Arriving at New York in December, and receiving aboard ample supplies of gunpowder, Price was sent orders to sail early in January, 1799.[62]

February 8, in the Gulf of Florida, the two cutters and their charge, together with four smaller merchantmen which they had taken under protection en route, welcomed the arrival of Stephen Decatur, Sr., in the 20-gun *Delaware*, because, at the time, a powerful 44-gun British frigate, the *Solebay*, was firing at them to bring to for boarding and examination. All hands at quarters, Decatur stoutly maintained that orders or no orders, Captain Rowiod of the *Solebay* couldn't trifle with American national ships, and offered to fight if the Englishman persisted in an attempt to dishonor the American flag. Rowiod was reluctant to breach amicable relations and to attack the inferior *Delaware*, assisted as she would be by two cutters, and the little fleet grandly sailed on for Havana.[63]

At this station, the *General Greene* shepherded American merchantmen to and from Cuba, without encountering any Frenchman until

March 6. Towards midnight, lying in company with the *Delaware* off Morro Castle, the cutter challenged a strange sail, which surrendered on the fourth shot hurled at her. Price discovered that he had taken the French privateer *Marsouin* of Cape Francois, a schooner pierced for 12 guns, but only carrying one brass 9-pounder, a crew of 26 men, and a cargo of 70 barrels of meat. The prize was worth about $4,000, and was sold for that, despite her captain's attempt to establish a character as a merchantman because his privateer's commission had expired.[64]

In May, the frigate *General Greene*, Captain Christopher R. Perry, was sent to relieve Decatur, who was to decide whether or not the cutters were worth retaining on the war duty.[65] Apparently, Decatur decided that the cutter *General Greene* was not suited to the Caribbean work, because Price arrived at Philadelphia about the middle of the month,[66] and on the 20th, Stoddert returned the cutter to the Treasury Department, because her 98 tons made her "too small to be useful in the Navy."[67] She finished the war, serving on the Atlantic coast.[68]

Price, however, was commissioned a naval lieutenant in July, and in September was given command of a naval schooner at Baltimore.[69]

The *"Pickering"*

The cutter *Pickering* was identical to the *Eagle*, differing only in having 4- instead of 6-pounder guns. She captured 5 Frenchmen, besides numerous American victims of the privateers. Built at Newburyport, Massachusetts, she was commanded by Captain Jonathan Chapman to January, 1799, Lieutenant Edward Preble (of Tripoli fame) to June, 1799, and by Master-Commandant Benjamin Hillar to the end of her service.[70]

Placed under the Navy's authority in a circular order of July, 1798, the *Pickering* sailed from Boston on August 22, in company with the *Herald*, 18, Captain James Sever.[71] Writing to Stoddert, Stephen Higginson, Navy Agent at Boston, remarked, "The Cutter also is well appointed, with good Officers & a good crew. Capt. Chapman is not inferior to any man in the Navy, many think to excell, & his officers are very good."[72]

The two ships beat uneventfully up and down the coast from Boston to Newport, speaking incoming or outgoing merchantmen, and an occasional British man-o'-war, such as the *St. Albins*, 64.[73] Putting finally into Newport, October 24, Captain Chapman discovered a Navy commission awaiting him, and in recommending Hillar to succeed him, summarized the previous months. "This cruise has been very unpleasant attended with much stormy weather, in which the *Pickering* has sustained some damage."[74]

This, certainly, was not a very brilliant beginning.

On November 4, the ships again put to sea in response to orders to go to Boston,[75] where Lieutenant Edward Preble, "said to be a valuable man," took over the *Pickering* in accordance with the privilege of choice between the two granted him by Stoddert.[76] Equipping the *Pickering* to join Barry, Preble received word to depart in the middle of January, 1799.[77] His orders contained what may today seem to have been a curious injunction.

> Being at peace with all other Nations, we should endeavour to cultivate, and preserve it, by practising the duties of Civility, and Friendship;—Should you meet with any American Vessel, captured by the Vessels of any nation at war; except the French or should you see any such vessels in the act of capturing an American vessel;—you cannot recapture in the one case;—nor can you lawfully interfere to prevent such capture in the other;—It must be presumed that the courts of such nation will render justice.[78]

It would seem that our government was mindful of our British bedfellows.

February 13, Preble left Nantasket Roads with the *Herald*, now commanded by Lieutenant Charles C. Russell, and a storeship destined for Barry's squadron.[79] The voyage was peaceful, according to the logbook of the *Pickering*'s sailing master, James Ingraham, who recorded legs of 60 to 163 miles, while the cutter kept a mile or so in the van of the other ships, busying her raw crew with the decks and rigging or great gun and small arms drill. The routine apparently caused John Thompson, seaman, to forget himself; after a reading of the Articles of War, he was "punished with 12 lashes for disobedience of orders and Insolent behaviour [sic] to the Master."[80] Making a landfall of Dominica at noon, March 13, the *Pickering* next day reported to Barry, after first suspiciously going to quarters upon sighting the squadron. Having only a few days' stores left and no base, Barry welcomed the addition to his force.[81]

Preble spent his first day in Prince Rupert's Bay with the cutter careened, while his crew "blackd the bends, and scrubb'd the Bottom down to the copper."[82] March 18, the *George Washington*, 24, Captain Patrick Fletcher, which had recently arrived, started out with the *Pickering* to take a group of merchantmen clear of the Indies. They looked in at Montserrat Roads for more Americans, and anchored the following morning in Basse Terre Roads, alongside the *Constellation*, 36, and her prize, the 36-gun *Insurgente*.[83] For a short time protected by the *Constellation*, the convoy sailed two days later. Hillar was occupied with pursuing strange sails, which usually proved to be flying the Stars and Stripes. After leading the merchantmen into relatively safe waters, the *Constellation* turned back, leaving Fletcher and Preble to take them farther to Latitude 27° N., where they were dispersed on March 27, Fletcher continuing on to Newport, while Preble headed back to Barry.[84]

Making a landfall of Antigua on April 14, Preble spoke a British man-o'-war, and three days later dropped anchor with the squadron in Prince Rupert's Bay. While watering—the cutter daily expended about 60 out of her 3,000-gallon capacity—Preble watched the *Constitution* and cutter *Eagle* take out a convoy. Leaving the Bay on the 20th, the *Pickering* cruised northwards, and while chasing a pair of ships past the southwest point of Guadeloupe, was saluted by three shots from a fort, one shot singing past the cutter's forefoot. Hoisting his colors, Preble fired back, and stood for Basse Terre. An hour later, he was fired on again by the defenses of Fort Royal, and thriftily returned a single shot, disappointed that the batteries kept him from investigating a pair of ships within their range. Towards dawn, he approached what he thought was the *George Washington*, and was surprised to find himself confronting a British ship-of-the-line whose captain truculently resented being challenged by a 14-gun brig. Preble prudently ran for Montserrat Roads where he found Fletcher, who had likewise encountered the two-decker.[85]

The next day, Preble discovered that the cutter's foremast was sprung some 14 feet above deck, but was able to bring her out of the Roads by the 26th. On the 29th, he intimidated a brig with three shots, and found that she was the *Fair American* out of New York with a prize crew of two Frenchmen and seven negroes aboard; she had been taken the previous day by three French letters of marque. On May 1, Preble fired seven shots to halt what he at first thought was a sloop, but which proved to be an 80-ton schooner whose foremast and boom had gone by the board in a gale. She was the *Francis* out of Fredericksburg, and a victim to a handful of Frenchmen. Undoubtedly, Preble was disappointed that her master had not been kept aboard but sent in a cartel to Guadeloupe, because her master had been his brother Joshua.[86]

May 6, the cutter's mainmast was sprung, obliging Preble to put into St. Pierre to fish it. From this port on the northwest side of British-held Martinique, Joseph Ingraham was dispatched in the cartel *Union* to carry 15 French prisoners to General Desfourneaux in exchange for any Americans at Guadeloupe, one of whom should have been Joshua Preble. Ingraham returned with 11 unfortunates, who were all he could find upon being invited to look in the streets and taverns for his compatriots, and he was chagrined not to have been able to get a receipt for his human cargo, since the French General had felt it would have been an admission of a state of war which everyone was anxious to disbelieve. At the same time, Preble corresponded with Captaine de Frigate P. Moreau, who had been his friend prior to the hostilities, but couldn't receive any better information on his brother's whereabouts than that Joshua had gone to St. Bartholomews, indicating, presumably, that he was free.[87]

At sea again, Preble looked in at various ports to advertise a convoy which he and Fletcher would take north. This group of 65 left St. Thomas on May 25, and was to have remained intact to Latitude 34° N., but broke up in heavy weather on June 9. On the 12th, the cutter was at Sandy Hook.[88]

During this cruise, she had recaptured two Americans, hailed or stopped 14 ships, including four British men-o'-war, and chased a score of strangers.[89]

Preble was promoted to Captain, and Hillar, his first Lieutenant, was given the *Pickering*. In sending Hillar instructions to go down to Guadeloupe, Stoddert wrote,

> I shall desire him [the senior officer on the station] to afford you every opportunity to distinguish yourself Officers and crew,— and not to employ a vessel so well calculated for cruising to advantage, in the more unprofitable business of convoying our Merchant Vessels.[90]

Stoddert's policy has already been mentioned, but he added an injunction that indicated the United States was beginning to feel its strength. In addition to being civil to representatives of all nations, Hillar was sternly reminded "that on no account you suffer the American flag to be dishonored."[91]

With dispatches for Tingey, Hillar sailed June 27.[92] Ingraham's logbook is missing as a source of information about this cruise, for he had somehow been made our chargé d'affaires in Tripoli.[93] On July 15, a few days after reporting, Hillar was sent with the *Ganges* and *Merrimac* on a patrol, and in their company recaptured the 57-ton schooner *John*, which was sent with a midshipman to St. Kitts.[94] During August, he cruised with the two ships, and on the 22d took a small convoy a day's sail north of St. Thomas, before taking over a beat to windward of Anguilla, where he could expect to find small privateers. By the month's end, Hillar was back at St. Bartholomews, his troublesome mainmast sprung again.[95]

In September, prize money began to come his way. On the 16th, he seized the *Atalanta*, a schooner laden with sugar, which was sold at St. Kitts for about £2,500. Towards the end of the month, before being relieved by Morris, Tingey decided to disperse his little squadron for the best possible protection to our shipping, and assigned the *Pickering* and *Delaware* to guard the passage from St. Bartholomews to windward of Nevis.[96] On this duty, the *Pickering* assisted in the recapture of the brig *Henrich*, and recaptured, by herself, the brig *Brothers*.[97]

The Federal Gazette and Baltimore Daily Advertiser of December 9, 1799, is the sole source for a description of another action:

> On Saturday last arrived the schooner *Gull*, captain Brightman, from Anguilla, who has favored us with the particulars of the following important victory.
>
> About the 18th ult. [October] off Point Petre, a battle was fought between the United States brig *Pickering*, of 14 guns, four pounders and 70 men, and the French privateer schooner *L'Egypte Conquise*, of 18 guns, 14 nines and 4 sixes, and 250 men; in which after an engagement which lasted nine hours, the Frenchman struck and was carried into St. Kitts.
>
> Captain Brightman, with many other Americans, had been previously captured by the above privateer; and it appears that she was one of the best vessels belonging to the French in the West Indies. She was completely fitted out and double manned, on purpose to take the *Pickering*; but not being able to stand the fire of American cannon, she was obliged to strike to a force not much more than one third her equal in number.
>
> The *Pickering*, a few days before, had a running fight with a French lugger; and capt. B. informs us, that she would have taken her if the *Pickering* had not sprung her masts in the chase.[98]

In November, Truxtun in the *Constellation* relieved Morris, and was emphatically directed to abandon the squadron cruising system. Results, insofar as the *Pickering* was concerned, began to be apparent the following month. On the 7th, Hillar took *La Voltigeuse*, a schooner of 10 guns and 64 men.[99] "It was expected that this privateer would have engaged the *Pickering*, as she shewed 14 ports; but on the *Pickering* firing a shot athwart her forefoot, and giving three cheers, the French colors came down." Ingraham suddenly reappears as the Lieutenant who boarded the prize, having been relieved of his job at Tripoli, for which he had little liking.[100]

Twenty days later, Hillar wrote a letter to Stoddert that, although in no sense as cryptic or gallant as Perry's message on an occasion of larger moment, nonetheless indicates the character of a Revenue Marine officer.

> *Pickering*, at sea, 27th Dec. '99
>
> SIR, Having this day fell in with, and captured a French privateer of 10 guns and 61 men, an occasion offering to inform you of the same, I pray you to excuse my not being so particular as I otherwise should be.
>
> I have the honor to remain, Sir, Your most obedient servant.[101]

Between August and December, the *Pickering* recaptured four other merchantmen; two Americans, an Englishman and a Dane.[102]

Early in December, the cutter as a cartel carried French prisoners to Guadeloupe, and secured the release of a hundred Americans.[103] Having fallen in with the *Insurgente*, 36, now commanded by Captain Alexander Murray as a vessel in the Navy, Hillar cruised with the frigate for a few days. They stopped outside of Pointe a Pitre, port of the island of Grande Terre, where a French frigate of 50 guns and a corvette of 20 had lately arrived. Finding them "snug under the fortifications," the Americans couldn't do anything to the potentially dangerous pair, but left them to the careful vigilance of British warships from St. Kitts, since the English were equally if not more anxious than the Americans to destroy the strong French craft. When the *Insurgente* and *Pickering* met the 24-gun *Connecticut*, Hillar went his way.[104]

The cutter was lying at anchor in Basse Terre Roads when Truxtun brought the *Constellation* in, January 21, 1800. Hillar was then sent out with another convoy of two-score merchantmen, and on February 2, recaptured the *Portland*, bringing her total prizes to 17, including the French schooner privateer *Fly*.[105]

April 24, Hillar took his last ship, *l'Active*, a privateer of 12 guns and 62 men, and shortly afterwards was ordered to Boston for repairs, where he arrived May 17, after successfully bringing 70 more merchantmen out of the Indies. The repairs were to be made as quickly as possible, for, according to Stoddert, "The *Pickering* is so useful a Vessel—and Hillar is so clever a fellow that I am anxious she should get out again without delay."[106]

A situation arising similar to that of 1898, when part of the fleet was immobilized because of possible Spanish raids, Hillar's orders were changed on June 2. He was to cruise along the coast, among other things, to "Shew yourself at Charleston just to let it be known that you are on the Coast."[107] Leaving on the 10th, Hillar made the cruise of showing the flag without incident other than damage to spars and sails, and on July 25, he was relieved of the detail and ordered to the West Indies, where, he was informed, "your presence is too essential."[108] He was to wait only to act as protector of the storeship *Florida* out of Philadelphia with supplies for the squadron.[109]

The *Pickering* sailed in August and never reached St. Kitts. Overdue, she was first feared lost, and then, at last, given up.[110] As the *Naval Chronicle* summarized it,

The *Pickering*, Hillar, having returned to the United States, and made a short cruise on the coast, was directed (15th August) to proceed to Guadeloupe, and cruise in that neighborhood, until she should fall in with the commanding officer. She proceeded on this service, but was lost, it is supposed, in the same gale with the *Insurgente*—the equinoctial gale of September, 1800. All the crew in this case, as in that of the *Insurgente*, perished.[111]

The *Pickering*, her officers and men, half Revenue Cutter, half Navy, should have a place in the traditions of both services.

Notes

1. *The Rise of American Naval Power*, by Harold and Margaret Sprout, Princeton University Press, 1939, pp. 25–49. *Our Navy and the Barbary Corsairs*, by Gardner W. Allen, Houghton Mifflin & Co., Boston, 1905. pp. 13–87. Cf., also, Allen's *Our Naval War With France, passim*.
2. *Quasi-War With France*, documents, edited by Captain Dudley W. Knox, U.S.N., in seven volumes, Washington, 364–73. Totalling guns for relative strength, regular naval vessels had a total of 881 guns, and the cutters, 152, a rough 15 per cent (VII, 364–73). Using James' system of determining regular strength by computing total broadside weight of metal, the cutter strength would be less than 15 per cent.
3. "*Les Colonies Francoises*," by J. Rambosson, Paris, Ch. Delagrave et Cie., 1868, p. 362.
4. *Quasi-War*, I, 336.
5. *Ibid.*, III, 199.
6. *Ibid.*, V, 378.
7. *Ibid.*, V, 379, IV, 378, *passim*.
8. *Ibid.*, III, 385.
9. *Ibid.*, II, 68–9.
10. *Ibid.*, VII, 366. *The History of American Sailing Ships*, by Howard I. Chapelle, W. W. Norton & Co., New York, 1935, p. 182.
11. *Ibid.*, VI, 276a.
12. *Ibid.*, I, 323, 430, 433.
13. *Ibid.*, I, 481, 483.
14. *Ibid.*, I, 528.
15. *Ibid.*, II, 49.
16. *Ibid.*, II, 81.
17. *Ibid.*, II, 222, 339. (This is one of the Coast Guard's present duties—suppression of mutiny at sea.)
18. *Ibid.*, VI, 276a.
19. *Ibid.*, II, 463–4.
20. *Ibid.*, II, 496.
21. *Ibid.*, II, 523; VI, 276a, 563–4.

22. *Ibid.*, III, 64–6, 73, 77.
23. *Ibid.*, VI, 276a.
24. *Ibid.*, III, 220.
25. *Ibid.*, III, 555.
26. *Ibid.*, III, 327.
27. *Ibid.*, VI, 276a; III, 327.
28. *Ibid.*, III, 129, 327.
29. *Ibid.*, III, 454.
30. *Ibid.*, III, 493.
31. *Ibid.*, III, 512–3.
32. *Ibid.*, IV, 47, 215.
33. *Ibid.*, IV, 133–4.
34. *Ibid.*, VI, 276a.
35. *Ibid.*, IV, 170–1.
36. *Ibid.*, VI, 276a.
37. *Ibid.*, IV, 432.
38. *Ibid.*, VI, 276a. *Record of Ship Movements*, U.S. Coast Guard, Washington, 1935, in two volumes. Vol. I, p. 95.
39. *Ibid.*, V, 103.
40. *Ibid.*, VI, 276a.
41. *Ibid.*, V, 227.
42. *Ibid.*, VI, 276a.
43. *Ibid.*, V, 411, 469.
44. *Ibid.*, VI, 276a.
45. *Ibid.*, VI, 73.
46. *Ibid.*, VI, 276a.
47. *Ibid.*, VI, 365.
48. *Ibid.*, VI, 366.
49. *Ibid.*, VI, 391, 430.
50. *Ibid.*, VI, 559; VII, 22.
51. *Ibid.*, VII, 58.
52. *Ibid.*, VII, 134–5.
53. *Ibid.*, VII, 241, 307.
54. *Ibid.*, VII, 367.
55. *Ibid.*, I, 210.
56. *Ibid.*, I, 221.
57. *Ibid.*, I, 256.
58. *Ibid.*, I, 272, 275.
59. *Ibid.*, I, 292, 295–6.
60. *Ibid.*, I, 538.
61. *Ibid.*, II, 95–6.
62. *Ibid.*, II, 200, 203–4.
63. *Ibid.*, II, 322.
64. *Ibid.*, II, 421–3.
65. *Ibid.*, III, 149.
66. *Ibid.*, III, 176.

67. *Ibid.*, III, 220.
68. *Ibid.*, III, 252.
69. *Ibid.*, VII, 345.
70. *Ibid.*, VII, 369.
71. *Ibid.*, I, 328; VII, 368.
72. *Ibid.*, I, 329.
73. *Ibid.*, I, 340 *passim* to 576.
74. *Ibid.*, I, 576.
75. *Ibid.*, I, 500; II, 6.
76. *Ibid.*, II, 66, 110.
77. *Ibid.*, II, 219.
78. *Ibid.*, II, 250.
79. *Ibid.*, II, 306, 346–7.
80. *Ibid.*, II, 440.
81. *Ibid.*, II, 306 *passim* to 474.
82. *Ibid.*, II, 473.
83. *Ibid.*, II, 486–7.
84. *Ibid.*, II, 499–500, 503 *passim* to 531.
85. *Ibid.*, III, 47, 64–5, 83.
86. *Ibid.*, III, 88–9, 99, 108, 116.
87. *Ibid.*, III, 147, 164.
88. *Ibid.*, III, 174, 225 *passim* to 257; 301, 321.
89. *Ibid.*, III, 633.
90. *Ibid.*, III, 252, 341.
91. *Ibid.*, III, 380.
92. *Ibid.*, III, 385, 500.
93. *Ibid.*, IV, 231.
94. *Ibid.*, IV, 93, 473.
95. *Ibid.*, IV, 44 *passim* to 83; 97, 120, 136–8.
96. *Ibid.*, IV, 195, 225–6.
97. *Ibid.*, V, 563.
98. *Ibid.*, IV, 295.
99. *Ibid.*, IV, 377–9, 500–1.
100. *Ibid.*, V, 137.
101. *Ibid.*, IV, 571.
102. *Ibid.*, IV, 589.
103. *Ibid.*, IV, 530.
104. *Ibid.*, V, 31.
105. *Ibid.*, V, 132, 137, 145, 212.
106. *Ibid.*, V, 374, 512, 528, 565.
107. *Ibid.*, VI, 4.
108. *Ibid.*, VI, 59, 179.
109. *Ibid.*, VI, 219, 226, 257.
110. *Ibid.*, VII, 120.
111. *Ibid.*, VI, 415.

2

"The Coast Guard Cutter *McCulloch* at Manila"

Captain Randolph Ridgely Jr., USCG

U.S. Naval Institute *Proceedings*
(May 1929): 417–26

IN JANUARY, 1898, the *McCulloch* sailed from Hampton Roads for San Francisco, via Suez Canal and the Far East.

Carnival week was in full swing when the *McCulloch* moored to an Admiralty buoy in Valeta Harbor, Malta. The British authorities, naval and military, were especially cordial, and officers and men were made to feel perfectly at home and joined heartily in the festivities of the week.

On the morning of February 17 the commanding officer received a dispatch from Washington informing him the *Maine* had been blown up in Havana Harbor the night of February 15, and shortly after this the governor general sent an aide on board to express the sympathy of his government and himself, and a copy of a dispatch he had received, giving many more details than had been contained in the dispatch from Washington.

Speculation ran riot on board and the probability of war was discussed and deemed a certainty. All hands were very much upset, as we were bound to San Francisco, and the general opinion was that if war was declared, all activities of any importance would be in the Atlantic and Cuban waters and we would be out of it. So several officers applied to be detached and ordered home so they would be available for duty on the Atlantic. Of course, no action was taken on these applications and as it developed, it was fortunate for those concerned, as they would have missed May 1, at Manila.

The British were more cordial than ever after the *Maine* tragedy and from kindness, a very amusing incident occurred. Certain naval officers had been detailed to see that the officers of the *McCulloch* were looked out for. Of these officers, two were lieutenants, one attached to the *Empress of India*, the other to the *Royal Oak*, sister battleships, moored abreast. The governor general's ball was given the night of February 21, and the *McCulloch* was to sail at 6:00 A.M., the morning of the twenty-second. At 2:00 A.M. we left for our ships. The two lieutenants were quite sure they must see us aboard, which they did, and it was thought they should remain until just before sailing time, which was unanimously agreed upon as being the only proper thing to do.

At 5:30 A.M. a boat was called away and our hosts and guests were returned to their ships, but unfortunately the officer from the *McCulloch* who put them on board got the officers and ships confused, and on struggling up two sets of the *Royal Oak's* gangway ladders with the officer from the *Princess of India*, was greeted by a marine sentry with—"Beg pardon, sir, this h'officer does not belong h'aboard." The situation was immediately grasped by the *McCulloch's* officer, who explained that it was "perfectly all right" and this officer was to occupy the cabin of the lieutenant who did belong "h'aboard," which he did.

The case was very simple, then; the *Royal Oak's* officer was placed aboard the *Empress of India* after practically the same conversation and procedure. Many weeks afterwards we received a most amusing letter from one of them describing how he had awakened the next morning, the cabin looked familiar, the gun room looked perfectly natural, but the photographs and souvenirs in the cabin he occupied were absolute strangers and unknown to him. When he rang for a servant and asked where he was, he was informed that he had been put aboard by an American officer.

Proceeding to Port Said, Suez, Aden, and Colombo, each day putting us farther from the scene, and at each port getting news which led us all to believe war was inevitable, we were in a rather low frame of mind. But things took on a brighter hue on arrival at Singapore when Mr. E. Spencer Pratt, American consul general, came on board with a dispatch directing the *McCulloch* to proceed with all possible speed to Hongkong and report to Commodore George Dewey, U.S. Navy, commanding the Asiatic Squadron, especially when other dispatches directed movements to be secret and to cruise without lights at night. It appeared we had missed these orders by only a few hours at Colombo.

Mr. Pratt, the American consul general, had made all arrangements for coaling, stores, etc., but due to the fact that the *McCulloch* had arrived after sundown Saturday, April 8, and that the following day was Easter Sunday, nothing could be done till Monday the tenth. We coaled and provisioned on that day and on the eleventh sailed for Hongkong and what was to prove our first experience with war.

The *McCulloch's* sailing from Singapore was delayed about eight hours due to a misunderstanding in regard to salutes. She arrived after sundown on the eighth and proceeded at once to a coal dock. The next day, Sunday, no salute was fired, so on the afternoon of the tenth, after coaling had been completed, the *McCulloch* dropped into the stream and fired a 21-gun salute to the British flag. Several hours elapsed before a return salute was fired, which was very unusual, as the British are very punctilious in such matters; then the salute was returned by eleven guns, this being noted at once and a letter dispatched ashore to the governor general, through the American consul general, asking why the salute was not returned gun for gun and requesting a proper salute.

It so happened that the governor general was up in the country, but the matter was taken up with his aide-de-camp, who informed Mr. Pratt that the *McCulloch* had only fired a salute of eleven guns, which they did not understand, but after consultation this salute had been returned gun for gun, and that was that.

Mr. Pratt then came on board to be sure of the facts in the premises, and found out we had fired a salute of twenty-one guns, with the white ensign at the main truck. Our commanding officer was all ready to sail, yet was reluctant to proceed until a proper salute had been returned. Mr. Pratt was also insistent that the *McCulloch* await the firing of a proper salute; he went ashore and brought the governor's aide-de-camp back with him, who explained no slight was or had been intended, that the governor general was not in Singapore and would not return till the next day, when he felt sure the salute would be fired as requested, and also it was so late then he would not be able to return ashore and order the salute till after sundown and they did not fire salutes between sundown and before 8:00 A.M.

The aide-de-camp was politely but firmly informed that our sailing orders would not permit of this delay, that we must demand the return of the salute gun for gun as regulations on this were positive and admitted of no discretion on the part of our commanding officer and under the circumstances he must insist on the salute being returned immediately. It was also suggested that as Joshua had commanded the sun to stand still till he finished a battle, "official sundown" could be delayed till the salute had been fired, then evening colors could be made and all would be shipshape.

Whether the reference to Joshua was appreciated or not, the salute was returned by a 21-gun salute, shortly after sundown, and evening colors made immediately afterwards. During the various discussions in regard to the salute, what really caused the mix-up was developed. It was a hazy morning with light airs blowing directly from the signal station; the *McCulloch* was lying broadside to the signal station and about a mile and a half away. The first gun of the *McCulloch's* salute was fired from the saluting gun trained shoreward, also the last. This made eleven guns observed, and heard, but apparently the offshore guns were not heard or observed owing to black powder being used, which made too much smoke to see about the ship.

Sailing from Singapore on April 11, we arrived at Hongkong the afternoon of April 17, and as the *McCulloch* steamed under the stern of the *Olympia*, some wag exclaimed, "Thank God, we are safe, the *McCulloch* has arrived." Nevertheless, the *McCulloch* proved an active and useful unit of Admiral Dewey's forces.

As soon as Captain Hodgsdon had reported and given Admiral Dewey all information in regard to the *McCulloch's* armament, speed, and personnel, orders were issued to prepare her as far as possible for any duty that she might be required to perform.

The *McCulloch's* battery of four 6-pounders was augmented by two 3-inch field pieces which were mounted on the t'gallant fo'castle, the engine-room force was increased by ten Chinese firemen, ship painted war color, coaled and provisioned, and men given intensive drills. War not having been declared, Admiral (then Commodore) Dewey took advantage of this fact to secure coal, supplies, and equipment, knowing that when war actually came, Great Britain would be strictly neutral and the nearest base would be seven thousand miles away, except Chinese ports where facilities were practically nil and supplies uncertain.

April 22, the *Baltimore*, which had been anxiously expected for several days, arrived with ammunition which was needed by all ships of the squadron, as none had their full allowance. All arrangements had been made for docking the *Baltimore*, cleaning and painting bottom; she was rushed into dry dock. On April 23 Commodore Dewey received from the governor of Hongkong, Major General Black, an official proclamation of neutrality, and a request that the American squadron leave the harbor of Hongkong not later than 4:00 P.M., April 25.

The afternoon of April 24, the *Boston, Concord, Petrel* and the *McCulloch*, with the collier *Nanshan*, and supply ship *Zafiro*, left Hongkong and proceeded to Mirs Bay, some thirty miles distant and in Chinese waters, to await the arrival of the other units of the squadron, which arrived April 25.

Commodore Dewey was not only impatient but incensed at the delay in the arrival of Consul Williams from Manila, yet he felt warranted in awaiting his arrival on account of valuable information which it was presumed he had obtained as to the strength, disposition, and preparation of the Spanish forces. Finally on the morning of April 27, a tug was sighted approaching the *Olympia* and it proved to have the consul on board. As soon as it was definitely known Mr. Williams had arrived, signal was made, "Prepare to get underway." When Commodore Dewey had obtained all information possible from the American consul, he sent him on board the *Baltimore*, and at 2:00 P.M. the squadron was underway for Manila, 600 miles away, and a naval victory which was to change the entire international policy of the United States.

Weather conditions were ideal but speed was determined by the slowest ship, the collier *Nanshan*, which prevented the squadron from making more than eight knots. Early in the morning of April 30, land was sighted, Cape Bolinao, and signal was made from the flagship for the *Boston* and *Concord* to scout Subic Bay. Later in the day the *Baltimore* was sent to support the first-named vessels. At about 4:00 P.M. the scouting force joined up again, and of course all were anxious to know what they had found. In a short time a signal was made, "All commanding officers report on board the flagship." It was then announced that no Spanish ships had been located and Commodore Dewey, who had only awaited this information to make his decision known and to give his final orders, did so with a brevity and terseness that was inspiring. These were his orders:

"We will enter Manila Bay tonight and you will follow the motions and movements of the flagship, which will lead."

There were no written orders. Some one remarked, "There was no discussion." Anyone who knew Admiral Dewey personally would be led to remark that this was a superfluous statement.

On the return of the commanding officer, Captain Daniel B. Hodgsdon, to the *McCulloch*, all hands were mustered, our orders made known, and translated copies of the proclamation of the Spanish governor general and captain general of the Philippines, and the Spanish admiral (which were anything but complimentary to the material and personnel of the American squadron; in fact the description of the personnel was positively insulting) were read. The morale, which was excellent already, became enthusiastic and as the men were piped down, three hearty cheers were given for the victory which to them was a foregone conclusion.

As the entrance to Manila Bay was only some thirty miles distant, the squadron remained hove to for some time and finally proceeded at reduced speed. No lights were shown except one small light aft so the ship astern could keep in column and maintain proper interval.

Visibility was good on the night of April 30; there was some moon, but it was partly cloudy. As the squadron approached Manila Bay, signal lights were observed and it was supposed we had been sighted either from shore or by scouting units sent out by the Spanish. No signals were made by Admiral Dewey, but about 11:15 P.M. it was evident the flagship had increased speed as the *McCulloch* had to do so to keep position. It was also apparent that we were entering the bay through Boca Grande and between Corregidor and El Fraile. This was an excellent piece of navigation and piloting as all lights for aid to navigation had been extinguished. At about 11:30 P.M. when the *McCulloch* had El Fraile on her starboard quarter, the first gun was fired from the Spanish battery of three guns mounted there. The *McCulloch*, *Boston*, and *Raleigh* returned the fire, the *McCulloch* firing only three shots, as we could not train sufficiently far aft to keep up the fire, and also because after firing three shots, the Spanish ceased firing, as did the *Boston* and *Raleigh*. In a short time all chances for the Spanish batteries on Corregidor and El Fraile to make hits on the squadron were over.

During the passage into Manila Bay through Boca Grande, the only casualty in the squadron occurred. The chief engineer, F. B. Randall, of the *McCulloch*, died from heat prostration superinduced by the excitement, and excessively high temperature in the engine room, which was recorded at 170°. Mr. Randall was a very stout man who took little or no exercise and this was only what was to be expected under the circumstances, but it did cast a gloom in the wardroom, as he was a good shipmate. He was stricken about 11:30 P.M., April 30, and was pronounced dead by Dr. Greene, surgeon, at 1:00 A.M., May 1.

Having accomplished the passage, the speed was again reduced and the squadron so maneuvered as to arrive off the city of Manila at daylight.

At a conference on board the flagship, Admiral Dewey had planned to hold the *Boston* in reserve, to protect the ships in line of battle from surprise attack and in case of any ship becoming disabled, to tow her out of range and take her place in line. The *McCulloch* was thus elected to take a position in the line of battle, but after it had been ascertained there were no Spanish ships at Subic, the conclusion was drawn that the Spanish had concentrated all of their major naval forces in the vicinity of Manila and, therefore, there would be little probability of a surprise attack, so Captain Frank Wildes of the *Boston* requested that he be permitted to take his ship into action with the squadron and the *McCulloch* be assigned the *Boston's* duties. The admiral acceded to this request and the *McCulloch* was ordered to follow the squadron into action keeping close watch on all ships, to be ready to tow any vessel that might be disabled or grounded out of line, and then take the disabled vessel's station, also to keep a sharp lookout for any surprise attack and protect the *Nanshan* and *Zafiro* from attack. These ships were to take a position well out of range.

May 1 dawned, a typical tropical day, scarcely a breath of air and a haze that resembled that which one observes arising from a hot steel plate; a fireman coming on deck for a breath of air described it perfectly, when he remarked to a seaman, "We people don't have to worry, for Hell ain't no hotter than this." As the squadron approached Manila, the only ships sighted were several square-riggers, merchant ships, and some steamers inside the breakwater and in the Pasig River. The squadron passed along the water front and then headed for Cavite. At about five o'clock the Luneta battery and other batteries of the Manila defenses opened fire, but the shots went wild. The *Boston* and *Concord* returned the fire, but fired only a few shells, probably out of humanitarian reasons, as their fire would probably have caused much loss of life among the noncombatant population of Manila. The squadron was drawing away in search of the Spanish naval forces and the target practice of the Spanish batteries was bad.

Shortly after 5:00 A.M., broad daylight, and the haze having been somewhat dissipated, the Spanish squadron was sighted apparently at anchor, close to Cavite arsenal and between there and Sangley point. About 5:20 A.M., the Spanish ships and supporting land batteries in the vicinity of Cavite opened fire. Most, if not all, the splashes were short, yet to many of the younger officers, who were impatient to begin firing, the next twenty minutes appeared ages. At 5:40 A.M. Admiral Dewey gave the order that has since taken its place so prominently in American naval history: "You may fire when you are ready, Gridley."

The first gun was one of the 8-inch from the forward turret of the *Olympia*. The action immediately became general and from 5,000 yards the range gradually decreased to 1,500 yards as we passed Sangley Point. All turns were on a port helm (right rudder) so that the starboard and port batteries alternately took up the fire on the Spanish squadron. Five runs were thus made past the Spaniards, three from eastward and two from westward. Because of the brown powder used and the light air stirring, visibility was poor, though the *McCulloch* had a wonderful front seat to observe this historical drama.

As the action progressed, it became evident that the admiral was closing in on the enemy at each turn till, on the final run, it was estimated by those on the *McCulloch* that the range had been reduced to about 2,000 yards. It was impossible to spot hits or splashes, but after the second run, it was very evident that fire had broken out on several of the Spanish ships, as the volume of smoke and the color indicated clearly it was not powder smoke; also flames could be noted shooting into the air. Of course enthusiasm increased as each burst of flame or explosion was noted and the *McCulloch's* crew became hoarse from cheering our ships as they passed.

As the range decreased and smoke increased, the visibility became lower and the *McCulloch* closed in to be in better position to see what was actually happening and to carry out promptly the orders in case of a casualty in our squadron. This caused another amusing incident. The Sangley Point battery had been forgotten or perhaps ignored and as we were following the squadron in one of its runs from west to east, a 4.7-inch shell splashed about fifty yards ahead. As we had orders not to fire unless we took station in the battle line, division officers were permitted to go on the bridge where they could see better. Lieutenant W. B. Elliott, U.S. Navy, who had been assigned to the *McCulloch*, in charge of the reserve squadron, remarked, "They (the Spanish) will never come that close again." Hardly had he finished when a shell passed over the *McCulloch's* bridge and the splash was spotted about 400 yards on our port beam. Every man on the bridge ducked below the canvas weather cloths, then gradually rose with a sheepish grin. Mr. Elliott, who had joined the "ducking party," remarked, "What the hell's the use of ducking; you'll never hear the whistle of the shell that hits you!" Again a shell from the Sangley Point battery passed over the ship, evidently much higher, nevertheless the "ducking party" was joined by all of those present. Shortly after this, division officers were sent to their stations and the rest of the action was seen from other points of vantage. Whether this was because a couple of the junior officers grinned in a manner that was a little more pronounced than a sheepish grin, has never been settled.

At 7:40 A.M. the squadron withdrew from action "for breakfast!" but as it actually developed, to check up on what ammunition had been expended and what remained, the casualties in the squadron, both in material and personnel, and to allow the smoke to drift away in order to observe the effect of our fire on the Spanish ships. A general signal was made, "Go to breakfast," and another, "All commanding officers report on board." As the several ships approached the *Olympia*, a casual glance showed no material damage had been done and it was argued that, therefore, personnel casualties could not be very heavy, though it was inconceivable that they should be so slight as were finally reported to the admiral: two officers, Lieutenant F. W. Kellogg and Ensign N. E. Irwin, and six enlisted men were wounded, all on the *Baltimore;* and though there were many close calls on other ships, these were all that were reported at breakfast that morning, though it later developed there were one or two officers and a few men who had been scratched by splinters or pieces of shell. Their names are not recalled, but there was much joking through the squadron when someone produced an imaginary wound.

It also turned out that the *Baltimore* was hit five times, the *Boston* four, the *Olympia* five (and a shell cut a signal halyard, just above the head of Ensign W. Pitt Scott and a quartermaster who were making a signal), and the *Petrel*, once.

At 11:15 A.M. the action was resumed, though by that time it was apparent that little or no further resistance could be expected as the Spanish ships were sunk, in flames, or had withdrawn into Bacoor Bay. The *Baltimore* led the second attack and concentrated her fire on the Sangley Point battery, the *Petrel* on the navy yard, the others on the plucky *Ulloa*, which soon sank, firing to the last. At 12:30 P.M. the Spanish flag was hauled down and the Battle of Manila Bay was won. Then came the mopping up procedure. Lieutenant E. M. Hughes of the *Petrel*, with a whaleboat and crew, went into Bacoor Bay and set fire to six ships of the Spanish squadron that had been scuttled and abandoned by their crews. The *Concord* shelled and destroyed the *Mindanao*, a large transport with a valuable cargo. The *Manila*, an armed transport, was found beached but in good condition. She was seized and eventually cleaned and put in commission. The *Petrel* was on the job in the second and last attack, shelling Cavite. Ensign G. L. Fermier, in charge of one of the 6-inch gun divisions, took his card out and wrote "With my compliments to Admiral Montojo," and stuck it on the base of a shell. The next day when the *Petrel* sent a landing party ashore to examine the navy yard, this card was picked up in Admiral Montojo's own office in the yard; the shell had hit the building, exploded, and practically wrecked it, so Fermier's card certainly arrived at its destination.

It was a busy afternoon for all hands; every ship was assigned a duty or mission and performed it. The *McCulloch* was assigned the duty of taking Mr. Williams, the American consul, aboard one of the British square-riggers, the *Buccleugh*, with a note from Commodore Dewey to the Spanish governor general and captain general of the Philippines, which Mr. Williams was to ask the master of the *Buccleugh* to take ashore and deliver to the British consul for final delivery and to await a reply. The squadron being near Cavite, the *McCulloch* steamed over to Manila and sent a whaleboat in charge of an officer with Mr. Williams, to carry out the mission. She then steamed out in the bay to bury our chief engineer. Mr. Williams did not like this at all and made some rather tart remarks about being left to the mercy of the Spanish, whom he evidently expected to send out and take him off this British ship. He said that if the Spanish ever laid hands on him he would be tortured to death.

The master of the *Buccleugh* delivered the note to the British consul but returned before it was possible to get in touch with the Spanish authorities. Mr. Williams was taken back to the flagship at 5:00 P.M. and at 6:15 P.M. the *McCulloch* was ordered to take position one-half mile off the mouth of the Pasig River to prevent any vessel leaving or entering. She remained there till the next morning. The only incident to disturb us occurred about midnight when a large launch was sighted approaching the mouth of the river from Manila. As all running lights were being shown, she was not fired on but was hailed, brought alongside and examined. It was found she had a Spanish officer on board with a communication for Commodore Dewey. This information was signaled to the flagship and the *McCulloch* ordered to let the launch proceed and report to the *Olympia*.

May 4 the *McCulloch* coaled ship from the *Nanshan* and on the morning of May 5 received signal, "Be ready to get underway at 1:00 P.M." Shortly before the hour designated, Lieutenant Commander J. B. Briggs of the *Baltimore*, Lieutenant Thomas M. Brumby, flag lieutenant, Pay Inspector D. A. Smith, fleet paymaster, Assistant Surgeon Charles P. Kindelberger, and Mr. J. L. Stickney, New York *Herald* correspondent, came on board for passage to Hongkong.

When the *McCulloch* sailed from the United States, Mr. Edwin Harden had been sent by Frank A. Vanderlip, Assistant Secretary of the Treasury, to make investigations of financial conditions in the Far East. His friend John T. McCutcheon had accompanied him. When war was declared these gentlemen had been requested by cable, Mr. Harden by the New York *World* and Mr. McCutcheon by the Chicago *Tribune*, to become correspondents for them, and to cover the American operations in the Far East. Mr. J. L. Stickney of the New York *Herald* was already at Hongkong. All three of these gentlemen had volunteered their services to Commodore Dewey and he had accepted their offer. Mr. Stickney, a Naval Academy graduate, served on Commodore Dewey's staff. Messrs. Harden and McCutchen were assigned to duty on the *McCulloch* and given charge of the powder division (the old berth-deck cavalry), and all performed their duties in a most creditable manner.

It was to be supposed that there would be keen rivalry among the correspondents to score a "beat" for their papers. There was, but Lieutenant Brumby left the matter to them with only one proviso, which was that no correspondent was to file or attempt to file his story with the cable people until his dispatches had gone through. He would then give them the word "go" simultaneously. This was the procedure and was followed out implicitly, but one of the correspondents secured a "beat" of a couple of hours by filing his story at "straight rates," which took precedence over those filed at "press rates." This was never confirmed but, if true, was perfectly legitimate, a clever move and the correspondent had a keen sense of news values.

At 1:00 P.M., May 5, underway, stood down Manila Bay, escorted by the *Boston* and *Concord*, as it was reported several Spanish men-o'-war were lurking in the vicinity of the entrance. As Boca Chica was opened, a large ship was sighted and the *Boston* made signal "Clear ship for action." On closing this ship she was found to be the French cruiser *Brieux*. Shortly after this, 3:15 P.M., the *Boston* made signal "Proceed on duty assigned." The *McCulloch* proceeded at full speed, encountering fine weather, and arrived at Hongkong in forty-nine hours, anchorage to anchorage, having logged 646 miles.

The British, especially naval officers, were astonished to learn of the outcome of the battle and could not believe the American casualties could be so slight, when the Spanish were completely annihilated, and were more than anxious to hear the most minute details. The *McCulloch* brought the first authentic news which the outside world received, though various reports had filtered through from the Spanish authorities before the cables were cut, which varied from both sides having suffered severe losses, to the Spanish claim that they had beaten off the American squadron.

The *McCulloch* sailed from Hongkong on May 8 at 2:35 P.M. and made the return trip in forty-eight hours and thirty minutes, logging 633 miles. Arriving at Manila on May 10, bearing the dispatch that notified Commodore Dewey of his promotion to rear admiral, the *McCulloch* coaled ship, and on May 13, departed for Hongkong again. We ran into the tail end of a typhoon on the last leg of the trip, taking fifty hours to make the run and logging 637 miles, anchoring this time in Korlung Bay, Chinese waters. On this trip we had on board Ensign H. H. Caldwell, one of Commodore Dewey's aides, and Mr. Alexandrino, an insurgent leader, who evidently was sent to Hongkong to get in touch with Aguinaldo, head of the insurgent movement.

May 17, sailed again for Manila with a number of passengers, among whom were Aguinaldo and thirteen of his leading supporters. Aguinaldo was a man of small stature; he was very quiet and conversed only in Spanish, though it was understood that he spoke English fluently; he was very reserved and so far as the *McCulloch's* officers were concerned, sought and gave no information.

May 19, arrived at Manila after a run of forty-eight and one-half hours, logging 639 miles. The insertion of time and distance in the various runs to and from Hongkong is simply to show consistently good navigating and steaming efficiency, the greatest difference in time between the longest and shortest period being two hours and thirteen minutes, due to heavy seas; the greatest difference in miles logged being thirteen, due to running off our course to intercept the *Brieux*.

After the second trip to Hongkong, the *McCulloch* was kept in Manila Bay by Admiral Dewey for boarding, patrol, and scouting duty, and as a general utility unit of the squadron. She lay with anchor short and with sufficient steam to get underway instantly. On signal to get underway we began to heave in and if she was not underway in three minutes from time of signal, the officer of the deck got his. This duty was interesting, amusing, and sometimes exciting, as all ships, man-of-war or merchant, were boarded, notified of the state of blockade, and informed as to what Admiral Dewey expected their procedure to be. All visiting ships of either class courteously and cheerfully followed out the procedure expected by our admiral except the Germans, and they either intentionally or through ignorance seemed in every manner possible to violate all ethics applicable under the circumstances. The *Irene* and *Cormoran* were constantly underway and were the most annoying of the German ships. On two occasions it was necessary to fire a shot across their bows to make them heave to, so they might be boarded, once at night by the *Raleigh* across the bow of the *Cormoran*, and once during day by the *McCulloch* across the bow of the *Irene*, when she ignored the international code signal, "We wish to speak you."

This last incident occurred off the entrance to Manila Bay with a heavy sea running. When she did heave to, the *McCulloch* sent an officer in a whaleboat to board her. The commanding officer of the *Irene* would not lay his vessel so our boat would have a lee, nor did he lower his companionway which was rigged out. Our boat was put along side and the officer boarded her by stepping out of his boat to the hammock nettings of the *Irene*. She was pretty high-sided, so one can imagine it was fairly rough. All the *Irene's* commanding officer had to do was to bring the sea a little on his port bow, which was easy as he was practically headed into it, to make boarding fairly easy. So the boarding officer was decidedly curt in asking where she was from, where bound, and also telling what Admiral Dewey expected the commanding officer to do on his arrival at Manila.

On June 29, received signal from the *Olympia*, "Spanish gunboat sighted bearing northwest apparently attempting reach Manila, intercept and capture." That time the *McCulloch* broke her record, getting underway in one minute; as soon as the anchor was aweigh she was going ahead full speed. A course was shaped to get between the gunboat and the foreign shipping lying off Manila. This was accomplished and we headed for her. She changed course to meet us head on. There was little or no breeze and it was seen that she flew a flag at the fore, pennant at the main, and a flag at the main gaff. Knowing the Spanish spirit, all hands thought she was determined to put up a fight. The younger division officers were anxious to begin firing, but Lieutenant Daniel P. Foley, who had succeeded to the command when Captain Hodgsdon had been ordered home, would not fire till he was sure of the intent of the enemy's vessel. On closing in on her, it was found she was flying a white flag at the fore. A boarding officer was sent aboard and found her to be the Spanish gunboat *Leyte* that had escaped from Manila the early morning of May 1, and taken refuge up one of the numerous rivers emptying into the bay, hoping to escape some night, but this had been frustrated by the vigilance of the American squadron. When the insurgents became more active, her commanding officer took fifty Spanish officers and their families on board and decided to come to Manila and surrender to the admiral.

The Spanish flag was hauled down, the American ensign hoisted and with a prize crew on board, proceeded to the *Olympia* and anchored on her starboard quarter. The *McCulloch* sent a whaleboat to the *Leyte* to take her commanding officer and the prize master to the flagship. In the meantime a heavy rain squall had kicked up quite a choppy sea; also that morning the *McCulloch* had coaled from cascoes, and despite a close watch some "bino" had gotten on board, so the crew did not pull in the style and form usual in Navy boats in those days. As the two officers approached and mounted the *Olympia's* gangway, some of the younger officers waved congratulations, so the prize master was a little doggy as he was ushered into the admiral's presence and said, "I have to report the capture of the Spanish gunboat *Leyte*, sir, and to deliver the commanding officer on board." The admiral said, "Very good, and I want to say your boat's crew pull like a lot of damn farmers." This incident shows that nothing went on in Manila Bay that Admiral Dewey did not see.

The squadron settled down to maintaining a strict blockade and preparing to meet a Spanish squadron consisting of the *Carlos V*, *Pelayo*, and *Alfonso II*, carrying 12.6-inch and 11-inch guns, which had been dispatched to wipe out the Spanish defeat of May 1, as well as the American squadron. This expedition had proceeded through the Suez Canal, anchored five miles off Suez, and coaled from its colliers. After the defeat of Admiral Cervera's squadron by Admiral Sampson's and a proposed demonstration by the American Navy against the Spanish coast, Admiral Camara reentered the Canal, and on July 11, sailed with his ships for Cartagena. This ended any possibility of Spanish naval activities in the Philippines.

From July 11 the American squadron awaited the arrival of American troops and were ready at any moment to cooperate with the Army in the capture of the city of Manila, which eventually fell August 13. During this long wait, one of the favorite sports of the American squadron was to count the number of refugee ships lying off Manila, estimate their value and figure how much prize money each officer and man would receive. It appears that the consuls of neutral nations had requested Admiral Dewey to permit them to charter some of the Spanish merchant ships that had taken refuge in the Pasig River on May 1, to place their nationals on board so they would be safe in case the Americans should find it necessary to bombard the city. The admiral granted this request provided the consuls would guarantee the surrender of the ships to him when the city was captured. The delay necessary for the Army to prepare for the attack postponed the capture of the city till the day after the armistice was signed, so the officers and men lost thousands of dollars, as these ships had to be returned to their owners.

The monotony of the regular routine, accentuated by the rainy season, and by the fact that visits between ships were permitted only during daylight hours, and then not encouraged, was broken by the arrival of troop ships. There were also frequent engagements between the Spanish and insurgents, and scouting trips in Manila Bay and along the adjacent coast. On August 7 the usual forty-eight hours' notice preparatory to the bombardment of a fortified city was given, and orders issued to the squadron to be ready for action the morning of the tenth. On August 9, Admiral Dewey sent word to the foreign war vessels and refugee steamers to shift anchorage so as to be out of the line of fire. The English and Japanese men-of-war came over near Cavite and anchored, while the French and Germans shifted anchorage to the northwest. That same afternoon the *Concord* and *Petrel* shifted anchorage to a position near the Germans, but on the morning of the tenth, the *Olympia* hoisted signal, "The attack is postponed." On the twelfth, the Army having finally completed its plan, it was announced the attack would be made next day.

At 8:45 A.M., August 13, the American squadron was underway. As it passed the *Immortalite*, Captain Chichester, senior British officer present, her guard was paraded and the band played. The *Immortalite* and *Iphigenia* then got underway and steamed between the American ships and the other foreign men-of-war, maintaining this position till the city surrendered.

The American ships took position as follows: *Charleston*, *Boston*, and *Baltimore* off the Luneta; the *Monterey* nearer the city proper; the *Concord* off the mouth of the Pasig; the *Olympia*, *Raleigh*, *Callao*, and the *McCulloch* near the Malote fort. At 9:35 a slow fire was opened on the Spanish fortifications and lines, as the Army was attacking from this direction. The fire was kept up for about an hour but was not replied to by the Spanish. It is now believed a matter of history that Admiral Dewey had an understanding with the Spanish commanding general that he would not fire on the city of Manila unless the Spanish heavy batteries opened fire on his ships. Of course, this was not known throughout the American squadron at the time of the attack.

When it was seen that our troops had entered the city via the Luneta, other troops were brought over in light-draft vessels and landed along the water front, the boats from the squadron being used for this purpose. While engaged in this duty, word came that the Spanish had set fire to a gunboat in the Pasig River. Ensign G. W. Bradshaw took two of his boats and two from the *McCulloch* to try to put out the fire and save her. It was apparently a hopeless task from the beginning and when what appeared to be a torpedo was found in the fore hold, Bradshaw ordered all hands to leave her. It appeared years before all men were rounded up and gotten into the boats. Bradshaw and the *McCulloch's* officer having mustered their men in the boats, they shoved off to await the explosion which never came. She finally burned to the water's edge and sank.

At 5:00 P.M., Admiral Dewey sent his flag lieutenant, Brumby, ashore with some signal boys and they hauled down the Spanish flag flying over the citadel and hoisted the American flag. All American ships fired a 21-gun salute, the bands played "The Star Spangled Banner," and Manila passed out of the hands of the Spanish. All foreign men-of-war present were notified that Manila was in the possession of the Americans and that the port was now open. Captain Chichester of the *Immortalite* acknowledged this by firing a national salute with the American flag at the main, this being the only foreign ship that did.

The Navy now placed all its resources at the disposal of the Army, handling stores, transporting troops, and assisting the troops in every manner possible. The *McCulloch* was very active in this work and the only break in these activities was an occasional trip along the bay and coast to investigate conditions or to secure such information as Admiral Dewey desired.

The last duty of any importance performed by the *McCulloch* was the capture of the "gun-running" steamer *Pasig*. It appeared the insurgents believed in preparedness and not knowing whether or not the Americans would concur in their policies in regard to the Philippines, they were securing arms. Admiral Dewey, being aware of this, gave orders to the American consul to be on the lookout and give him prompt notice of any war material whose probable destination was any place in the Archipelago. During the latter part of September he received a cable saying the *Pasig* was sailing from Macao with rifles and ammunition bound for Batangas. The *McCulloch* was ordered to intercept and bring the *Pasig* into Manila. Though the *McCulloch* proceeded immediately and steamed faster than the *Pasig* could, the steamer was found anchored at Batangas, both anchors down, no fire under her boilers, and no one on board. She was boarded at once and searched; only a few sporting rifles and shot guns were found on board. No ship's papers or other documents were found to determine the nationality of the vessel. These facts were reported to Captain C. L. Hooper who was in command. He sent a hawser and a prize crew on board with orders to get both anchors up and ready to be towed. While this was being done, several boat loads of Filipinos came off and were allowed on board. Two men claimed they were agents of the ship, but no one admitted being either officers or members of the crew. Captain Hooper permitted them to remain on board as his orders directed him to expedite the mission. Within two hours the *McCulloch* was proceeding with the *Pasig* in tow. The prize crew began to get steam, and in four hours the *Pasig's* engines were turning over. The next day the *Pasig* was delivered to Admiral Dewey. It was then learned that after the *McCulloch* had sailed, information was received that Batangas was strongly fortified by the insurgents as one of their bases, and they intended resisting the capture of the *Pasig*. This had worried Admiral Dewey, as the *McCulloch's* battery consisted of 6-pounders only, so he was greatly relieved on her return. If there was any truth in the rumor, the rapidity with which the *McCulloch* accomplished her mission took the insurgents by surprise and they were evidently not prepared to resist.

On November 11, the *McCulloch* was detached from the Asiatic station and directed to proceed to San Francisco, her original destination, touching at Hongkong, Amoy, Shanghai, Nagasaki, Kobe, and Yokohama en route. On this occasion Admiral Dewey, in his letter to the Secretary of the Navy reporting the detachment of the *McCulloch* said, "and now beg to state that all duty assigned to the *McCulloch* was performed with the greatest zeal, efficiency, and judgment."

Though the duty was often monotonous and climatic conditions not conducive to comfort, all hands felt keen pangs of regret at leaving. Many new friendships had been made and old ones renewed. Every man was proud to have played a part, be it ever so humble, in one of America's greatest naval victories.

3 "Armaments and Gunnery in the Coast Guard"

Commander R. R. Waesche, USCG

U.S. Naval Institute *Proceedings*
(May 1929): 381–84

IN THE DISCUSSION of armaments and of gunnery efficiency in the Coast Guard, or the fighting ability of Coast Guard vessels, the history of the service may be loosely divided into three periods, viz., (1) from the inception of the service in 1790 until the close of the Civil War; (2) from the close of the Civil War until the entry of the United States into the World War; and (3) from the entry of the United States into the World War until the present time. During the first of these periods vessels of the service were heavily armed and their fighting efficiency was high and increasing. During the second period the number of guns carried by vessels was gradually decreased with correspondingly less attention paid to gunnery. The third period has witnessed a marked improvement in the ordnance equipment of Coast Guard vessels and a revival of interest in the preparedness of the service for war.

Under the Act of Congress approved August 2, 1790, the first ten cutters of the service were constructed, all heavily armed. Eight years later, five of these vessels, together with three of more recent construction, were ordered to duty with the Navy for operation against the French in the West Indies. The *Pickering, Eagle, Governor Jay,* and *Virginia* carried fourteen guns each and the *General Greene, Scammel, Dilligence,* and *South*

Carolina carried ten guns each. Later the number of guns on the *Scammel* was increased from ten to fourteen, though this vessel had a displacement of but ninety-eight tons. This West Indian fleet was composed of twenty vessels and included the historic *Constitution* and *Constellation*, and among its officers were Barry, Truxtun, Nicholson, Preble, and Stephen Decatur. It is particularly noteworthy that no change was made, nor was any necessary, in the armament of the revenue cutters when they were temporarily relieved from carrying out their normal peacetime duties and assigned to duty with the Navy, and this condition was generally true throughout the history of the service prior to the close of the Civil War. The seagoing arm of the Treasury Department consisted of heavily armed craft and needed no additional armament when operating with the Navy as they did on many occasions. The number of guns of heavy caliber that these vessels carried is surprising indeed. The *Surveyor*, a cutter of less than seventy-five tons, in commission during the early part of the nineteenth century and very active with naval forces during the War of 1812, carried as her peace-time armament eight 12-pound carronades, and this was a typical armament for cutters of that class.

The normal duties of the service in this early period were such as to require a maximum fighting ability. The suppression of piracy, the prevention of smuggling, the breaking up of the slave trade, the enforcement of neutrality, all required a display of force, and desperate engagements were not infrequent. In 1819, the cutters *Louisiana* and *Alabama* were boldly attacked by the pirate ship *Bravo*, commanded by Jean LaFarge, a lieutenant of the notorious Jean LaFitte. The pirate was finally boarded and captured after a furious hand-to-hand encounter. Later the *Louisiana* captured and destroyed the pirate *Bolivia* though the latter vessel had more guns and carried twice the force of the cutter. Engagements of a similar nature occurred frequently throughout the early history of the Coast Guard.

In those days it was unnecessary to use artificial means to stimulate interest in gunnery. Competition, cash prizes, qualification pay, trophies, and the like had not been introduced nor were they needed. Men of such vessels as the *Eagle, Jefferson, Gallatin, Vigilant,* and many others were trained to fight by fighting. The stimulus to gunnery efficiency for officers and men alike was the defense of their ship and their lives, the pride of victory, the glory of conquest.

After the close of the Civil War the gunnery efficiency of the service gradually declined as the everyday need for fighting ability became a thing of the past. As the cutters became larger the armaments became smaller, not only relatively but actually. Vessels of two or three times the size of their predecessors carried half as many guns and these guns were little used. Piracy in the Western Ocean passed into history; slave traders no longer had a market for their human cargoes; smuggling by force gave way to smuggling by stealth. While the duties of the service increased with the development and expansion of the country, particularly with the purchase of Alaska, they rarely necessitated a show of force, and actual fighting was extremely rare.

At the outbreak of the Spanish-American War the cutters were hastily fitted with guns commensurate with the size of the vessels, but immediately upon the declaration of peace the heavier guns were removed and the smaller-caliber guns reinstalled. The general apathy toward ordnance and gunnery was resumed. Cutters of a thousand tons carried a maximum armament of four 6-pounder guns while a hundred years before cutters of one hundred tons carried ten to fourteen guns of similar size. Consequently, previous to 1917, Coast Guard personnel had very little training or experience with modern naval guns, and were unfamiliar, as a rule, with the gunnery exercises prescribed for naval vessels. While target practices were occasionally held in this prewar period, they were conducted in a more or less desultory fashion. It is true, of course, that Coast Guard vessels were greatly handicapped in their gunnery training work as the manifold duties of the small force of vessels kept them busy throughout the year. The weekly gun drills, however, were regularly carried out, though at times these were more or less perfunctory. No attempt was made to inaugurate a modern fire-control system or to train personnel in fire control or spotting. At the outbreak of the World War, which automatically placed the Coast Guard under the operation and control of the Navy Department, Coast Guard vessels were rushed to navy yards, the smaller batteries removed, and 3-inch and 4-inch guns installed. Upon the declaration of peace and the return of the Coast Guard to the Treasury, most of the 3-inch and 4-inch guns were retained aboard the cutters. Since that time a marked improvement in the attention given to ordnance and gunnery in the Coast Guard has taken place.

In 1921 four new vessels, the *Haida, Modoc, Mojave,* and *Tampa,* were built for the Coast Guard and provisions were made for carrying on these vessels three 5-inch 51-caliber guns, one 3-inch 50-caliber anti-aircraft gun, and two 6-pounders. This is the normal armament for this class of vessels and all guns are permanently installed except that during times of peace only two, instead of three, 5-inch guns are carried. The foundation for the third gun is in place and all that is necessary to install the third gun is to bolt it to the deck. The magazines are designed to carry the war-time allowance of ammunition for all guns. This was a radical departure in the ordnance policy of the Coast Guard, as it was the first time Coast Guard vessels carried modern guns using other than fixed ammunition. Regular drills and exercises as prescribed for naval vessels of this class have since been thoroughly carried out.

In 1924, Congress authorized the transfer of twenty destroyers from the Navy to the Coast Guard and in 1926 five more were transferred so that the Coast Guard now has in service twenty-five destroyers organized in divisions similar to Navy practice. Twelve of the destroyers are of the so-called one-thousand-ton type, armed with 4-inch 50-caliber guns, and thirteen of the seven-hundred-forty-ton type, armed with 3-inch 50-caliber guns. These vessels each year, after preliminary training, fire short-range battle practice, day spotting practice, and long-range battle practice as prescribed for destroyers in the current edition of "Orders for Gunnery Exercises," except that no torpedoes are fired.

In 1926 Congress authorized the construction of ten new Coast Guard vessels. Five are completed and have been recently commissioned. Their war-time armament consists of three 5-inch 51-caliber guns and two 3-inch 50-caliber antiaircraft guns. The foundations for the guns are built in and the magazines arranged to carry the full war-time allowance of ammunition. These vessels now carry one 5-inch 51-caliber gun, one 3-inch 50-caliber antiaircraft gun and two 6-pounders. The 6-pounders are carried on the 3-inch gun foundations and one 3-inch gun is carried on a 5-inch gun foundation. In addition thereto, the vessels are equipped with a dual fire-control telephone system with anti-noise telephones and battle control panel approved by the Navy Department. Bids for three more cutters of this program will shortly be solicited and the plans for these vessels call for the same armament as the other five. The magazines will be constructed in accordance with plans approved by the Navy Department and will include a handling room with separate compartments for the different calibers of ammunition, flooding and sprinkling systems operated by group control valves, ventilating system and other modern features. The magazines will be insulated.

All Coast Guard destroyers and first-class cutters are equipped with the Ford range keeper, Mark II. With the exception of the five newest cutters, Coast Guard vessels are equipped with the 1-meter, Mark XXI Barr and Stroud, or the 1-meter, Mark XIV Bausch and Lomb range finders. These instruments have not proved entirely satisfactory and they will be replaced by larger instruments as soon as practicable. The five cutters commissioned during the past six months have been supplied with 3-meter range finders, Mark IV, and while this is one of the older types of range finders in use in the Navy, good results should be obtained with it.

For the destroyers and, where available, for first-class cutters, the Navy regulation battle raft is used for battle practices. Arrangements have been made with the Navy Department whereby one of the battle rafts at Hampton Roads is lent to the Coast Guard. The Norfolk Navy Yard keeps the raft in repair and supplies all the necessary equipment and material for rigging it, the cost being borne by the Coast Guard. This battle raft is now at Charleston, S.C., where Coast Guard destroyers are holding short-range battle practice, day spotting practice, and long-range battle practice.

There are now in service in the Coast Guard thirteen 5-inch 51-caliber guns, forty 4-inch 50-caliber guns, fifty-five 3-inch 50- caliber guns, nine 3-inch 50-caliber antiaircraft guns, forty-eight 3-inch 23-caliber guns, forty-six 6-pounders, and 259 1-pounders. All guns, range finders, and range keepers are the property of the Navy Department; they are lent to the Coast Guard. This is a sound policy, for guns of 3-inch caliber and above as well as all fire-control equipment are placed on board Coast Guard vessels for Navy use in time of war and for training personnel for the Navy for war-time employment. When Congress by appropriate legislation transferred twenty-five destroyers from the Navy to the Coast Guard, the act authorized the transfer of all armaments as well. However, in order to continue the uniform policy of the title to guns on Coast Guard vessels resting with the Navy, the guns of the destroyers were placed in the same status as other guns aboard vessels of the service and formal transfer of ownership of the armaments was not made. The General Board of the Navy is always consulted regarding the proposed armaments of Coast Guard vessels under construction and its recommendations followed. It is in accordance with such recommendations that 5-inch guns have been placed on all first-class Coast Guard cutters built since 1920 and that fire-control equipment has been furnished without cost to the Coast Guard other than preparation and handling. Coast Guard vessels have no need of this equipment for carrying out their normal peace-time duties and except for war-time employment would not be so equipped. The cost of repairs, maintenance, and upkeep, as well as the replacement of spare parts for all guns and equipment, is borne by the Coast Guard.

Until a few years ago, the Navy furnished the Coast Guard ammunition without charge in accordance with the basic policy of having Coast Guard units, as far as practicable, in a state of preparedness for war. Due to depletions in the stock of reserve ammunition of the Navy, this policy has been altered so that now the Coast Guard pays for all ammunition except the original supply of service ammunition which is kept on board for Navy war-time use. With modern guns up to five inches in caliber, good fire-control equipment for small vessels, adequate voice tubes and fire-control systems, and the regular Navy allowance of target ammunition for the battle practices prescribed for Navy vessels of similar class, the ordnance and gunnery material of the Coast Guard is in excellent shape.

As an incentive to the enlisted personnel to attain excellence in gunnery, the Coast Guard has by law the authority for the payment of cash prizes to gun crews, and the rules and regulations governing the payment of such prizes follow the precedent established by the Navy. Likewise, Coast Guard enlisted men are entitled to qualification pay for gun captains and gun pointers in accordance with Navy standards, and a number of men in the Coast Guard are now drawing this increased compensation.

In order to keep our warrant gunners thoroughly conversant with improvements in modern guns and the latest practices in the repair, upkeep, and maintenance of ordnance material, the Navy has generously instituted a course of instruction at the Washington Navy Yard for Coast Guard warrant gunners. The course is four months long and includes instructional work in each shop and department of the Washington Navy Yard, including the optical shop. All warrant gunners of the Coast Guard must take the course. Four gunners compose a class and upon the completion of the course by members of one class they return to their regular duty and a new class is immediately assembled.

For the past three years four Coast Guard commissioned officers, usually one lieutenant commander or commander and three ensigns or lieutenants (junior grade), have been assigned to duty with the Navy Scouting Fleet during their maneuvers and exercises in the Guantanamo-Gonaives area. This association with naval officers while carrying out the prescribed battle practices has been invaluable to the development of modern gunnery in the Coast Guard and it is hoped this practice will be an annual custom. Unfortunately, the shortage of commissioned personnel in the Coast Guard does not now permit a larger number of officers to be detailed to this duty. For a number of years it was the practice to assign two Coast Guard officers to each class at the Naval War College, but due to shortage of commissioned personnel no such assignments have been made for several years. It is hoped that this practice may soon be resumed.

The greatest deterrent to excellence in gunnery in the Coast Guard lies in the many demands upon the service occasioned by its numerous and arduous peace-time duties. Gunnery training and practices must give way, necessarily, to the work of the Coast Guard in saving life and property on the high seas. With an inadequate number of commissioned officers, engaged in many important lines of activity, it follows that only a portion of a Coast Guard officer's time can be devoted to gunnery training and to the study that is necessary to prepare himself for efficiently training his men and for carrying out a well-conducted battle practice. Of course, gun drills are held at least twice weekly, spotting drills are held frequently, and the vessels, in going in and out of harbors, or passing lightships and vessels at sea, often hold brief drills or target approaches. Naturally, a commanding officer who is not especially enthusiastic over gunnery training can readily find excuses for not having his unit as well trained and drilled in gunnery as it is along other lines. On the other hand, an officer who is keenly interested in the gunnery efficiency of his vessel manages to find the time to train his personnel and to carry out a successful battle practice. It is not surprising that the scores made at battle practices and the proficiency with which such practices are conducted vary greatly, reflecting, as they do, the interest the commanding officer takes in the matter of gunnery training. The situation in general has been markedly improved by giving each cutter twenty days and each destroyer thirty days annually for intensive training in gunnery and for holding the prescribed battle practices, relieving the vessel during that period of all other duties, except that of responding to calls for assistance. While the

Coast Guard is not yet fully satisfied with the results being obtained, the progress is most gratifying. In several cases during recent short-range battle practices, 100 per cent hits were made and rapidity of fire showed continual improvement.

Excellence in gunnery in the Coast Guard may be developed in the same way as excellence is developed in any other line of endeavor. The outstanding requirement is the proper management, indoctrination, and inspiration of personnel. When the commanding officer's interest is keenly aroused, he is in a position to stimulate active interest in his subordinates, and proficiency follows as a matter of course. The efficiency of any unit, and the proficiency of its personnel, are directly dependent upon the qualities of leadership displayed by the commanding officer.

4 "The First Around-the-World Flight"

Chief Boatswain M. A. Ransom, USCG

U.S. Naval Institute *Proceedings*
(November 1938): 1589–1600

IN 1924 IT TOOK THE UNITED STATES ARMY world flight aviators nearly 6 months to fly around the world. It took them a month to traverse the shores of our own Alaska. They were in no hurry, had no speed records to break. They were scouting, experimenting in the sky world, studying ways and effects of nature, testing out devices, the flying tools which man's invention so far had given them.

The passage of those four planes was much heralded at the time. The accumulation of flying history since has so thrilled and advanced the thoughts of people about flying that one seldom hears now of that first mass flight around the Northern Hemisphere. This episode of 14 years ago is significant in that it was the first of its kind, an experimental trailblazer. It was not as spectacular or glory making as the Lindbergh flight 3 years later. But it may have been more useful to the trade.

This article deals with the Alaskan phase of the flight so far as the Coast Guard cutter *Haida* is concerned. That vessel departed from Bell Street dock, Seattle, April 6, 1924, on its annual cruise to the Bering Sea; but in addition it had orders to assist the 4 army planes, which, it was purposed, should fly over the Aleutian Islands on their passage westward.

The *Haida* steamed to Seward, Alaska, where a deck cargo of gasoline in drums was taken aboard for use of the planes, together with spare pontoons, a spare motor, and a pair of spare wings which might be needed in case of casualty. The vessel then stood for Unalaska, arriving there April 11.

There wasn't an officer or a man on board who was not thrilled at the prospect of adventure. Each had a keen eye laid for a picture that smacked so keenly of the dramatic—the first flight around the world! Planes zooming over the jealous seas, seas which heretofore had tolerated only ships, and not always them.

Advance agents for the flight had planted 4 buoys—gasoline drums painted yellow—in the narrows around from Unalaska up toward Captain Harbor. There the planes were to land on their way westward. The hills were still jacketed in snow, except where the blustery winds had blown them bare. The barometer read high, then low; rain, snow, gales, and squalls presaged only difficulty for the fliers when they arrived. For now we had received word that they had taken off from Seattle, and daily radio reports came to us of their passage. I shall use the personal pronouns "us" and "we," for each of us considered it a very personal affair, no matter what his station.

Then one Saturday, April 18, about 4:00 P.M., 3 planes appeared over Mount Ballyhoo, circled down, and landed in Dutch Harbor—a mistake; they had not seen the buoys. Again they took the air, passed over the watching townspeople and vessels' crews, found the buoys, landed again, and made fast. What, we asked ourselves, about the fourth plane?

The 4 planes which had started on the flight were numbered 1, 2, 3, and 4, named the *Seattle, Chicago, Boston,* and *New Orleans,* respectively. Number 1 was missing, the plane flown by Major Martin, the senior officer of the squadron. His plane had developed engine trouble in Chignik Bay, and would be along the next day.

We waited. By radio flash we learned that the missing plane had taken off. The few hours needed for the flight to Unalaska passed. It did not appear and we began to fidget. Night came—no news. At midnight the *Haida* cast off her lines and stood up toward Unimak Pass to search. The *Algonquin* from Chignik was searching from that end. We ran the 200 miles to the Shumagin Islands, peered into likely bays and waterways, found nothing. The assumption was the missing plane had grounded somewhere on the Alaskan Peninsula. So the *Haida* returned to Unalaska and there took up the duties of mothering those 3 planes and the 6 fliers on them who had got that far in their precarious adventure. And we continued in that role for the better part of a month—a month of elemental vagaries with little patches of brightness in between. It was into these bright intervals that the fliers had to fit their piecemeal journeying.

The fliers lived on the cutter. A watch was stationed day and night over the planes to guard against mishap. The notorious willie-waws of the region swept down the mountain sides and in through the narrows from seaward. The first night the *New Orleans* dragged its moorings, was saved from destruction on the rocky beach by the boat's crew on guard. Next day the *New Orleans* and the *Chicago* were brought around in front of the town and hauled out on the beach for minor repairs and to insure them from such further dangers. The *Boston* was landed on the dock by the steamer *Brookdale*, where the new engine we had brought from Seward was installed. It was all casually done. There was no hurry. The weather was bad. The weather man who traveled on the *Haida*, and whom we dubbed the heavenly soothsayer, sent up his little trial balloons, made adverse reports day after day.

Like a pall, anxiety as to the fate of Major Martin shrouded this activity, touching everyone. We wondered. Could he be safe? Had he hit the water? Had he been lost in the bleak mountains of the mainland? If he showed up, he would carry on with the flight. If not—kismet! the flight must go on.

One night about 10:00 P.M. the guard at the planes came running along the gravel beach toward the *Haida*, yelling. The searchlight playing on the planes brought all hands on the run. Continuous high winds had rolled up excessive high water. Now the sea was creeping in, washing the planes from their skids. By dint of hours of labor, men working in water up to their waists, the skids were cleared, the planes hauled higher up the beach. Again the *New Orleans* was the greatest sufferer from the storm.

On May 1 the *Haida* left for Atka, westward among the Aleutians, ran into a gale, hove to for a night, to be there when the planes came. For, with little likelihood of the lost fliers being found, the remainder had orders to proceed. And at last the weather man was predicting flying weather. When we arrived there the planes lay at the buoys. They had flown in a few hours what it had taken us two days to travel, what with gales and heavy seas. The fliers had missed the gale. The sky was loaded with storms. They had managed to fly in between them. The weather man with his balloons was doing good after all.

Now they were down again, safely moored to those yellow can buoys planted there for them ahead of time by the fisheries tender *Eider*. The process of watching and waiting would be repeated. The weather man had gone on to Attu in the *Eider* to send up his balloons, reporting conditions by radio. The first report showed boisterous weather out there. Fog lay over the sea and around the rocky shores. Not good flying conditions, not safe for landing. It was fair weather at Atka. Then we got good reports from Attu, but at Atka the old storm god had taken the elements in his teeth. So back and forth we joggled with wind and fog and sea, waiting for suitable flying conditions at both ends of the line.

Men could not fly, so they played and the *Haida's* crew played with them. Fishing parties ranged up the valleys in the fountain streams, hunters climbed the crags in search of eagles, while the more studiously inclined studied ethnology, using the slow-witted Atka natives for subjects.

Since the *Haida* was bound on a trip whose duration in days could not be estimated, the question of fresh water arose. The personnel were put on water rations. The vessel had 90 people on board. The tanks were limited. The evaporator ate up fuel. And as fuel was also related to the length of the trip, and because the oilers were almost human in their demand for fresh water, the problem became like a two-edged sword. A fresh water stream gushed down the mountainside out of the snow peaks in the distance. And so all boats were lowered. We ran a fire hose up the stream, snaked the other end to one of the boats anchored off the beach. So to work, back and forth, boat after boat, until the ship's tanks were full again. A bit old-fashioned, but the water question for the time was answered.

May 9 the day dawned ideal. At 4:00 A.M. calm prevailed. Rifts in the heavy clouds showed where the sun was about to break through. A breeze sprang up, freshened, then came daylight, and the swells began to ripple along the *Haida's* freeboard.

NOTE: *The following section appeared in the original magazine in a different font and tense from the rest of the article with no explanation as to why the shift.*

There is commotion, preparation, expectation. Boats are lowered away after breakfast, carrying parties of workers and observers. About 9:00 A.M. the three planes are seen taxiing out from behind the rocky islands lying between our anchorage and the inner bay. They circled round as if seeking some sort of formation, then the hum of their engines rose to a rumble while the smoke of their exhausts fanned up in great clouds behind them, to the awe and wonderment of the natives who had gathered on the top of the hill behind their village to watch the departure of these new and strange visitors. Hum, go the planes across the bay for a mile or so. One lifts and clears and circles over the land, then a second; but the third, the *New Orleans* again, ceased to rumble, went round in a ring, could not rise. The *Haida* manned and lowered a lifeboat. But it was not needed. For the plane now picked up and soon the huge bird and its man fliers rose clear of the sea. The trio of planes circled round the ship, lifting higher and higher. They waved good-by [*sic*], then turned in squadron formation and set a course up the valley between two high mountains. They soon vanished in a cloud.

The *New Orleans,* we learned later, had hit an air pocket and nearly went into a tail spin.

By this time the *Haida* had her anchor up and was headed for the open sea. When we arrived off Attu the planes were riding safely to their buoys in the inner harbor. Again we housed the fliers, serviced their planes. Servicing the planes was a ticklish job. If the wind was blowing the light-winged craft swayed and swooped on their mooring lines. A pulling boat would lay up to them from leeward, tail on to the fuselage; then running a small hose to the plane, pump gasoline into it from a drum in the boat. A pulling boat was better than a motor boat for handling near a plane. Men could lay on their oars, hold the boat steady. A motor boat was a vacillating body, which didn't ease the airmen's minds considering the uncertainties of the wind and a fluttering pair of wings— one bump and a wing or pontoon was out of commission. So it seemed to them; for those fliers were the "skeeredest people in all creation" when anybody or anything came near the planes with a possibility of damaging them. Each aviator was always present to supervise the fueling of his own plane.

At Attu word came of the safety of Major Martin, of how he had hit a mountain in a dense fog, how he and his mechanic had lived for days on little or nothing, walked many miles, nearly perished, and finally got into Port Moller. And we all breathed easier. The gloom departed. The expedition did not seem just right with disaster in its wake.

Early on May 15 the *Haida* got under way, shaped a course for the Commander Islands, leaving the aviators sitting in their cockpits, ready to go. At noon they took off. In a short while they passed over us, circled the ship in a last signal of farewell, then faded in the midday sky. That was the last we saw of them. They landed at the Commanders, but by the time the *Haida* got there they had taken off for the Kuriles. We went back to our summer cruising duties; they, as we know, spent the next three months over oriental cities and plains; partook of European welcome; crossed another ocean; then home again. But not so for the *Boston,* which went down in the North Atlantic and was rescued by a man-of-war.

The day the *Haida* returned to Seattle in the fall, the fliers arrived at that place, the end of their journey. And to celebrate they were housed again and feted, and they were given a chance to sample another meal such as they had enjoyed while trying to negotiate the murky Bering wastes.

5 "Reminiscences of World War Convoy Work"

Captain William J. Wheeler, USCG

U.S. Naval Institute *Proceedings*
(May 1929): 1313–22

THE VARIOUS COAST GUARD CUTTERS automatically became part of the United States naval forces upon our declaration of war, and assumed the duties assigned by previous instructions. These cutters performed a variety of duties, mainly in American waters, until August, 1917, when the *Manning, Algonquin, Yamacraw, Tampa, Seneca,* and *Ossipee* were designated for overseas duty, to be based on Gibraltar. The first to reach Gibraltar was the *Ossipee,* on August 30, 1917, and the next was the *Seneca,* on September 4, 1917; the others arrived after brief intervals.

For a few weeks these cutters were assigned to duty as Gibraltar Danger-Zone escorts, protecting freight convoys bound from or approaching Gibraltar. Beginning the latter part of October, 1917, the six cutters were assigned to duty as ocean escorts for freight convoys plying between ports in the United Kingdom and Gibraltar, where these convoys were made up again, en route to and from Mediterranean ports. Thereafter, the cutters performed ocean-escort duty almost continuously until the signing of the Armistice, this duty being interrupted only by an occasional brief individual Mediterranean trip, and by the loss of one cutter, the *Tampa,* with all hands, September 26, 1918, through action of an enemy submarine in Bristol Channel. Sharing this ocean-escort duty were the light cruisers *Chester* and *Birmingham,* and the gunboat *Sacramento.*

A Gibraltar Danger-Zone escort usually accompanied each convoy for some thirty hours after sailing, generally leaving the convoy under cover of darkness the second night out. A "Home Waters" Danger-Zone escort generally accompanied the convoy for a longer period on sailing from a port in the British Isles. Usually, but not always, a Gibraltar escort joined the convoy approximately a day before reaching Gibraltar, and a "Home Waters" escort invariably joined the convoy before reaching ports in the United Kingdom.

To avoid collision with convoys from opposite directions, and to deceive the enemy, routes widely divergent were employed, with the result that the normal sailing distance between Gibraltar and the British Isles was greatly increased. This, with the extreme slowness of the convoys, gave the trips a duration of from seven to twelve days.

Usually only one ocean-escort vessel was assigned to each freight convoy, which consisted of from six to thirty vessels. A British officer, assigned as commodore of the convoy, sailed on a freight vessel in the front line and was generally the senior officer present.

Just prior to sailing there was held a conference of the masters of freight vessels and the commanding officers of escort ships at which all details were explained; and there was distributed to each written instructions, including a diagram of the convoy, giving names and positions of all vessels, and the height of mast of each, for the better keeping of positions by means of sextant angles.

It is to be borne in mind that approximately six army corps were being supplied with food and munitions of war from the British Isles by means of these convoys; that the Allied freight vessels had all operated some three years without essential repairs, with corresponding loss of speed; that the personnel of the Allied merchant marine had suffered sadly from the war; that the routes of these convoys were hazardously near the German submarine bases; and that the speed of a convoy is that of the slowest vessel. The slowest convoy which the writer personally recalls made an average speed of five and one-quarter knots, and his fastest one made slightly over nine knots.

This freight convoy system was newly established when the cutters arrived at Gibraltar, and the difficulties associated with its early history cannot be overestimated. Darkening ships at night was all-essential and flashlight signaling and radio communication were necessarily reduced to cases of extreme necessity. The unfamiliarity with the system by merchant marine personnel of various nationalities, and the low speed and poor maneuvering qualities of the vessels, made position keeping very difficult, especially at night without lights and practically without communication. This was still more difficult in thick weather. The one signalman assigned to each freight vessel was not always proficient, so the megaphone or international code were in frequent demand.

The usual position for the ocean escort, especially at night, was zigzagging across the front of the convoy at distances of from 600 to 800 yards. This had the effect of keeping the front line of vessels (heads of columns) in fair alignment, but it necessitated the utmost vigilance on the part of the officer conning the escort ship and utmost confidence in the steering gear, necessarily overworked by constant zigzagging. The usual distance between columns was from 400 to 800 yards, and between ships in column, 400 yards. Prior to leaving the danger zone, escort duty on the flanks or astern of a newly formed convoy was even more irksome, owing to the greater confusion and scattering of vessels in the first part of the trip. The difficulties of the task of trying to round up not infrequent stragglers by turning back off the convoy flank, finding the missing vessel, steaming alongside and hailing her with megaphone—this on a dark night without lights—can more easily be imagined than described. These difficulties were greatly increased by the early practice of the occasional timid master of working out of the body of the convoy after nightfall and take position off its flank column in order that the dangers of collision to his own vessel might be reduced. The zealous patrol boat standing back and clinging to the flank column to avoid losing touch in darkness was very liable to be suddenly confronted by a specter in the form of a truant vessel looming up ahead with no running lights to indicate which was the safest way to shift the helm. Close shaves were too numerous to mention, and the nervous tension experienced by a zealous skipper of a patrol boat during hours of darkness and thick weather was extreme. Why more patrol boats were not sunk in collision is a mystery.

However, it was remarkable how soon improvements were to be noted. Especially noticeable was the difference between the first and last part of a single convoy trip. Naturally, many of the inherent difficulties could never be overcome, but the degree of adaptability soon shown, and the proficiency developed under extreme difficulties, constitute a tribute to the personnel of the British merchant marine which made up the greater part of these convoys. In this connection, I would observe that many of the commodores of convoys were of the Royal Naval Reserves rather than the Royal Navy; and these reserve officers were invariably masters of merchant liners who had long been members of the R.N.R. Surely, I have never met a higher class of officers and gentlemen, nor finer seagoing men.

Collisions between vessels of the same convoy were not infrequent in the early stages of this duty, and they were liable to occur later under conditions often prevailing. I recall a sinking from this cause on my first trip to England, and many instances of damage to vessels. Tragedy and comedy were often grimly intertwined.

Once, on a thick night early in December, 1917, the *Seneca*, zigzagging in front of the convoy, received the following laconic message from the master of the British steamship *Sahara*, which was directly ahead, in column, of the Italian steamship *Tortona*: "That Italian astern has run into me and cut my stern bulwark down to the deck." This was immediately followed by another message, "We find one Italian on board. We don't know what's become of the rest." This was promptly followed by a message from the *Tortona*, "*Senuka* [*sic*] come quick!"

The task confronting the *Seneca* of steaming around the flanks of a scattered convoy of twenty-three ships and reaching the scene of possible disaster under the thick weather conditions prevailing was not an easy one. However, by good luck and reasonably good seamanship, we hope, the *Seneca* maneuvered around the convoy to a position opposite the *Tortona*, ascertained that she was still floating and keeping an approximate position, and stood by her until daylight. Daylight revealed the flag of the *Tortona* half-masted in token of the loss of her second officer, who proved to be the refugee on the *Sahara*. Just how the second officer reached the *Sahara* has never been explained. The writer recalls the reply of a canny Scotch skipper who was hailed by megaphone with the query as to when he could get up more speed and get into position: "I dinna ken, I dinna ken. This ship is nae liner; she is an auld box."

On another occasion a Russian skipper, at the convoy meeting immediately preceding the sailing, explained through the interpreter that he could not promise to carry out the orders regarding suppression of all lights; that every order which he passed on board must first be approved by the soviet commission, and he was not at all sure that they would approve of the order regarding lights. He was assured that if his vessel showed any lights she would be promptly sunk by gunfire, and this apparently carried conviction even with the soviet commission.

The work taxed to the utmost both the fine maneuvering qualities and the recognized seagoing qualities of our small cutters, especially in the winter season with its long nights, and frequent fierce gales on this run. The crews consisted of a nucleus of Coast Guardsmen of the old school, filled in by enthusiastic young recruits—many of them, college men seeking early action and probably attracted by the one year's enlistment which, however, we were authorized to extend for long periods. These quickly became all that could be desired for the duty. Unfortunately, the law did not permit the young men of the Coast Guard to compete for commissions until just before the Armistice; otherwise, certainly we would have lost some of our young college men through promotion.

Amateur theatrical performances held in Gibraltar early in the war revealed an astonishing amount and variety of talent from the Coast Guard. A performer from the *Seneca*, whose services were often requisitioned, both in Gibraltar and in the British Isles, was an ex-cowboy, a lariat artist with considerable experience on the stage. He had also had experience on a square-rigger and he had been a trainer of horses for the French prior to our entry into the war. The writer recalls his first exhibition in Gibraltar when a British officer, watching the whirling rope, remarked, "Marvelous, marvelous! I have never seen anything like that before. You see I have never been in the States." When this man's year's enlistment expired he requested an interview with the commanding officer and cleared up a mystery long lurking in the latter's mind. The cowboy requested personal advice: should he request that his enlistment be extended, or should he reenlist for another year? "Between us," he said, "I lopped off fifteen years to get a chance to fight under the good old flag, and I don't want to take chances on being sent home now that we are getting so much action!" His enlistment was extended without official comment.

A system of subcaliber target practice established by Lieutenant Commander Jack, and proving to be highly satisfactory, was much used while on ocean-escort duty. A boat-hook staff was attached by means of a bridle to the wire of the deep-sea sounding machine; one end of the staff was weighted so that with about two hundred fathoms of sounding wire paid out, the other end of the staff would ride about a foot above the water. On this end was secured a tin can to simulate a periscope. Zigzagging on the flank of the convoy, the after guns' crews while regularly at their stations were practiced for hours at a time in good weather by firing at this improvised periscope, with subcaliber ammunition. Systematic shifting of crews gave all gun crews the necessary practice. When opportunity came for regular target practice off Gibraltar, the results were most gratifying to us as well as most surprising to the British who were assisting.

The *Seneca* and, we believe, each of the other five cutters in the War Zone, were at first equipped with four 3-inch guns, but in the summer of 1918 these were replaced by 4-inch 50-caliber, 1918 model guns, adding greatly to the efficiency of the batteries and the confidence of the crews. In the case of the *Seneca*, this new gun installation was made at Davenport Yard, Plymouth, by night and day work, with only a slight change of convoy routine.

After adoption of the convoy system, the alarming number of sinkings fell off immediately to almost none, thus indicating the material and moral effect even of an imperfect and undeveloped system of convoy. Later, attacks and occasional sinkings from convoy occurred, both in the vicinity of Gibraltar and the United Kingdom, with Danger-Zone escort accompanying the convoy, and also, at sea, with only the ocean escort protecting. Probably one-half of the attacks were unsuccessful. Since usually only the wake of the torpedo, the feather of the periscope, or a brief glimpse of a conning tower was to be seen, naturally false alarms occurred, both by day and night. In the Mediterranean convoys, attacks and sinkings were more frequent. On two short Mediterranean trips there were at least two bona fide attacks and one sinking, the latter in March, 1918.

The writer recalls two sinkings from a badly scattered convoy the first night out from Gibraltar, when the *Seneca* was still doing duty with the Gibraltar Danger-Zone escort, prior to her detail as ocean escort, which was October 19, 1917.

The above cases and three subsequent ones, to be described later— namely, those of the *Cowslip*, *Queen*, and *Wellington*, constitute the only sinkings that the writer recalls from convoy with which the *Seneca* was associated. The *Seneca's* convoy record, probably an average one, shows that she was either ocean escort or one of the Danger-Zone escorts for some thirty convoys, with an aggregate of some 580 freight ships.

During the period in which the *Seneca* was employed in convoy, a total of some twenty-one alarms concerning submarines, or their imminent proximity, were made to the convoy, either by the *Seneca* herself or some other vessel, only one of which was then proved to be false—the case of a dead whale sighted at a distance, floating on his side with belly partly exposed, and strangely resembling a submarine partly submerged, with the wake showing. Concerning the other twenty alarms, evidence is given in the official reports of the sighting of submarines, their periscopes or wakes, or the wakes of torpedoes in thirteen cases; thus leaving but seven cases in which the convoys were alarmed and where the actual presence of the enemy was markedly in doubt in the minds of those present. The *Seneca's* general alarm was sounded on other occasions when developments were not considered sufficiently serious to warrant alarming the convoy.

The experiences of the *Seneca* were probably typical of those of ocean-escort vessels in general, but she was fated to catch more than her share of attacks—for what reason no one can tell unless it be that she was known to be the slowest cutter.

The *Seneca* herself was believed to be the subject of attack in three or four instances, torpedoes passing quite close. She fired at submarines, their conning towers or periscopes, or what was believed to be periscopes, in six instances, and in eight other cases she used depth charges against what was believed to be a submerged submarine.

In one instance in the Mediterranean, following the use of a barrage of depth charges by our vessel, unquestionably a quantity of oil appeared on the surface. In another instance at sea, the officers believed that another explosion followed our use of depth charges. The *Seneca* dropped over one hundred 300-pound depth charges, and not infrequently the electric lights of the cutter were broken by the resulting detonations.

As a typical case of alarm, on November 26, 1917, on our third trip as ocean escort, off the Bay of Biscay, with convoy from Gibraltar to Plymouth, the conning tower of a submarine appeared on the port bow of the convoy some 2,000 yards from the Seneca, which was zigzagging ahead; this at about 1:30 A.M. In accordance with established doctrine, the after guns' crews fired at once, dropping two shorts very near the submarine, and she disappeared.

On the afternoon of April 24, 1918, on our tenth trip as ocean escort, with convoy of twenty-four vessels from Milford Haven to Gibraltar, the Gibraltar Danger-Zone escort having already joined, H.M.S. *Chrysanthemum*, on the flank of the convoy, attacked and probably sank a German cruiser submarine, first sighted under the surface by the lookout at the masthead. The general rejoicing was destined to be clouded that night by the sinking of the British sloop *Cowslip*, through a torpedo exploding directly underneath her wardroom, with a loss of five sleeping officers and the wardroom steward. This occurred at 2:45 A.M., April 25, 1918, astern of the convoy, with the *Seneca* zigzagging approximately a quarter of a mile away. The night was thick and I was already on the bridge. Orders then existing forbade the closing of a torpedoed ship. Therefore, a strict interpretation of these orders would have meant leaving the surviving officers and crew to their fate. However, traditions of the sea and of the Coast Guard prevailed, and the *Seneca* rescued the two surviving officers and the seventy-nine enlisted men from the sinking vessel and her boat and life rafts alongside; this just before the final plunge of the *Cowslip* some forty-five minutes after the explosion of the torpedo. The captain and the officer of the deck, both of whom were on the bridge, were the only officers who survived.

Characteristically cool was the attitude of the survivors of this tragedy. Mingled with the sound of hissing steam and the cries of the injured came the sound of their gun as they fired at the submarine which appeared momentarily on the surface. They immediately signaled the approaching *Seneca* with flashlight, saying "Look out! The submarine is near." They secured the depth charges at safety, this under extreme difficulties, to prevent damage to other vessels, coolly lowered their only boat, put over the life rafts and, in perfect order, slid down into the *Seneca's* boat, the skipper leaving the ship just as she was disappearing.

Lieutenant F. W. Brown, wearing only his pajamas and revolver, handled the *Seneca's* lifeboat, and veteran Boatswain Patterson, with the *Seneca's* crew, manned the *Cowslip's* boat after taking aboard her first load from alongside. Both were commended for coolness and excellent boat-manship in successfully rescuing, in the darkness, choppy sea, and cross currents, some sixty-five men. The majority were taken off the sinking vessel, which was practically broken in two by the explosion, the stern settling, and the bow hanging high in the air, on which the survivors took temporary refuge. Lieutenant Brown's modest report tells of holding the boat with oars, bows on, keeping her close enough to receive the men sliding down a line, and yet avoiding being swept under the forefoot by the strong cross currents as the doomed vessel arose and fell with the seas. This incident, and others to follow, fully justified the efforts that we had made to maintain a standard of boat efficiency with our crew, even though we were in the war zone and not primarily bent on saving life.

Lieutenant Brown made two trips with the *Seneca's* lifeboat, taking all who remained on board the second time, twenty-two men, which with his crew was far beyond the usual capacity of the lifeboat used. The *Cowslip* sank a few seconds after the last man reached the lifeboat.

Later developments proved that three German cruiser submarines were bound for the Mediterranean, one of which was probably destroyed by the *Chrysanthemum*; one sank the *Cowslip*; and the third was sunk in the Straits of Gibraltar by a 60-foot motor launch carrying only two depth charges, each 300 pounds.

The *Seneca's* next thrilling experience came four days later, a day after joining, in the Straits, our fastest convoy (nine knots), and the only one in our experience that did not stop in Gibraltar en route to the United Kingdom. While zigzagging in front of the convoy, the officer of the deck of the *Seneca*, the ever alert Lieutenant Brown, sighted a torpedo approaching from the port side. He immediately gave the order, "Hard astarboard," and the vessel was swung just enough to avoid the torpedo, which passed not more than fifty feet ahead of her stern. "Hard aport" was now necessary to avoid the oncoming convoy, and a second torpedo fired at closer range passed immediately underneath the *Seneca's* stern. Apparently proximity saved the vessel. The comment of a passenger, Captain Cornwell, R.N.R., who on hearing the general alarm, reached the deck in time to see the second torpedo approach, showed characteristic British humor, "Wheeler, I felt my hat go six inches straight into the air."

On her fourteenth ocean trip, with a convoy of twenty-four large vessels, on June 28, 1918, two days after leaving port, the large and stately British steamship *Queen*, flagship of the convoy, was torpedoed at 7:45 A.M. and sank in four minutes, carrying down the commodore of the convoy, Captain V. deM. Cooper, R.N., all the officers of the vessel except the third mate and a junior engineer officer, and nearly half the crew.

Lowering the three boats was attempted. One capsized; another, said to contain the commodore, captain and mates, was caught under the wing of the bridge and carried down; the third was lowered with a very few men, manifestly unskilled boatmen. Approximately twenty of the crew were precipitated into the cold water where they clung to bits of wreckage and to the overturned boat.

The *Seneca*, zigzagging ahead of the convoy, was immediately brought about and stood down to the scene between the oncoming columns of ships, passing signals being given to avoid collision. Wreckage shooting to the surface was disregarded, and ring lifebuoys and a small life raft, with lines attached, were thrown over as the *Seneca* steamed alongside the men struggling in the water. The *Queen's* boat was instructed by megaphone to pick up other survivors near it and to stand by.

Lieutenant Brown, called from his watch below, once more attired in pajamas and armed with revolver, again took charge of the *Seneca's* lifeboat, which was lowered in spite of floating wreckage.

In the meantime, all four guns were manned, shells were fired into the water, in clear spaces between ships, to convince the enemy that he was being bombed from various parts of the convoy.

Six men were rescued from the vessel; eight more, isolated, were picked up by the *Seneca's* lifeboat, and thirteen by the *Queen's* boat. As soon as it was observed that all men were out of the water, depth charges were dropped to discomfit the submarine, and the *Seneca* steamed alongside the *Queen's* boat and received the occupants at once by means of side netting always kept lashed to the rail. Our lifeboat with its occupants was quickly hoisted and we rejoined the convoy, which continued to Gibraltar without further attack.

The loss of Captain Cooper was peculiarly sad since this was the fifth trip on which the *Seneca* had been his ocean escort and no vessel had previously been lost.

The conservatism of the German submarine doctrine was apparent from this sinking. With twenty-three large freight ships still in the convoy, protected by one cutter, the submarine failed to follow up the attack.

On September 13, 1918, the *Seneca* left Milford Haven with a convoy of twenty-one vessels, and at 11:30 A.M., September 16, off the Bay of Biscay, the British collier *Wellington*, leading one of the columns, was torpedoed in the forepeak and almost immediately abandoned by her merchant crew. It appears that this vessel had been torpedoed before, and was making her first trip following repairs in dry dock; that the crew was entirely new; and that master and mate were violently opposed to leaving the vessel but were practically carried off by the crew.

The *Seneca*, again zigzagging ahead, proceeded at full speed in the direction of the torpedoed vessel, at the same time dodging fleeing vessels, since the convoy in this instance scattered badly. At 11:31 A.M. a lookout on the *Seneca* reported the conning tower of a submarine in sight on the starboard quarter of the *Wellington*, having apparently dived under the latter vessel after firing the torpedo. Three shots from the *Seneca's* 4-inch battery and several shots from other ships were fired at the conning tower, four of them coming fairly close; whereupon the submarine submerged and was not seen again. The *Seneca* dropped a number of depth charges, eight in all, as opportunity was presented to drop these without endangering vessels of the convoy; and numerous shells were fired from our 4-inch guns into clear spaces of the water to convince the submarine that he was being bombed from various parts of the convoy.

Three boats loaded with the crew, forty-five men in all, were seen pulling away from the *Wellington* while the *Seneca* was engaged in dropping depth charges, and a semaphore message was received from the master in one of the boats stating that he thought his ship would remain afloat, but that his crew had refused to remain by her; and he requested that help be given him from the *Seneca*.

Lieutenant Brown, the *Seneca's* navigating officer, immediately requested permission to lead an expedition to salvage the *Wellington*. I announced that I would order no one to such a desperate enterprise but would consider the matter of volunteers. As this news spread from division to division a great many volunteered, including Machinist W. L. Boyce, who offered to take charge of the engineer's contingent. Lieutenant Brown and Machinist Boyce were authorized to make a hasty selection from the daring volunteers, eighteen of the various required ratings being chosen. "Smiling" Jimmy Nevins, first class boy, seventeen years old, begged to be allowed to go.

The *Seneca* received the occupants of the *Wellington's* boats by means of rope netting on either side, the *Seneca* volunteers scrambling into one of the boats as the deserting crew came out. It was then that the vigorous urging of the master, mate, and assistant engineer induced eight members of the *Wellington's* crew to return with these officers.

This gallant band went aboard the deserted ship, from whence the meager protection of the *Seneca* must be quickly withdrawn to protect the fleeing convoy, and the story of their struggle against an adverse fate in attempting to save this vessel is one that should never die—certainly not in the minds and hearts of those at any time associated with the Coast Guard.

By the audacity of their move they had convinced the submarine that the *Wellington* was a mystery ship. No other explanation can be given for the failure of the submarine to renew the attack, especially in the half hour required to get up steam.

Stations had been assigned as they rowed to the *Wellington*. Each man speedily took up his designated post. The gun's crew stood by for further attack; lookouts took stations. Machinist Boyce hastily and ably took charge in the engine room. Every contingency within their means was provided for. Steam was ready in half an hour, and the vessel headed for Brest, the nearest Allied port. To keep up steam the *Seneca* men voluntarily and cheerfully took turns in the fireroom, whence escape would have been impossible in the event of further attack, or in the event of the sudden failure of the bulkhead forward of the fireroom. Each man worked with a will and disregard of danger that surpasses sober comprehension.

Ere long a speed of seven knots was reported. They had virtually won from the enemy, by sheer nerve. The destroyer *Warrington* had been dispatched to their aid, and finally success seemed to be in sight.

But the gallant enterprise was fated to succumb to the forces of nature. They were overtaken by a severe gale which forced them to stop because their course brought the gale astern, flooded forward compartments, put the vessel down by the head, and, in spite of every possible feat of seamanship, she refused to steer to leeward. The water gained gradually in the forward compartments, and the single lifeboat was lowered with the two mates and a merchant crew, with instructions to hold on to the sea painters until the rest of the crew could slide down the falls into the boat, which was then to hang on by the painter to leeward.

Unfortunately, Lieutenant Brown was called to the radio room at the critical moment, and the bow painter was cast off in the boat, with the *Seneca*'s men already sliding down the falls. Worse still, the stern painter was then cut in the boat, against orders. The boat drifted to leeward; the merchantmen proved to be poor oarsmen, and could not pull back to the *Wellington*. The boat finally went alongside the *Warrington* to leeward and was crushed in going alongside. The *Warrington* was unable to lower a boat in the seaway.

The *Wellington* sank in inky darkness, in the cold, angry waters of the Bay of Biscay, at 3:30 A.M., September 17, 1928, with the master, engineer, and three of the *Wellington*'s crew, Lieutenant Brown and Machinist Boyce, and seventeen enlisted men from the *Seneca*.

Even in the face of desperate conditions, the sublimest courage, fortitude, and resourcefulness were displayed. Lieutenant Brown energetically signalled with a flashlight to the destroyer for assistance until the decks submerged under him. Jimmy Nevins observed at the last moment that Lieutenant Brown was neglecting his own safety, and performed the task of removing the officer's rubber boots while he still signaled. Machinist Boyce at great risk performed the hazardous feat of bleeding the boilers to prevent serious final explosion. All calmly jumped into the black and turbulent water, after bidding each other good-bye, well realizing that their life preservers and such floats as they had been able to improvise could not long save them.

The *Warrington*, deeming it impracticable and an added hazard to attempt to pick up the men in the darkness with existing sea conditions, waited until daybreak and then saved what she could by steaming alongside and picking them up individually, by means of lines. Of the nineteen *Seneca* volunteers, eleven perished in the chilly waters; the remaining eight, including Lieutenant Brown, were rescued by the *Warrington* more dead than alive, some four hours later. The merchantmen who went into the water all perished. Of the *Seneca* lost, ten were of the Coast Guard, and one, Gunner's Mate Paul Marvelle, was of the Navy, temporarily serving on the *Seneca*.

The consistent heroism displayed by each man from the moment of volunteering until the rescue of the surviving minority is almost unparalleled even in the history of the World War. I quote from Mr. Fraser Hunt of the New York *Tribune*: "Of all the brave deeds done in this War none were finer nor more courageous."

The deeds of individual heroism were too numerous to recount. Coxswain James Clarence Osborne, after four hours in the water, sustained a shipmate and saved his life. Another *Seneca* man, not fully identified, all but gained the deck of the *Warrington*, to be thrown back by the sea five times. When finally exhausted, he called out with a wave of his hand, "Never mind me—get some of the others. Good-bye."

Nearly all of the *Wellington's* survivors had served a year or longer in the submarine zone and had been steeled in the schools of hardship and adversity.

The two recognized British naval historians, Messrs. Hurd and Bashford, in a brief joint history called "The Heroic Record of the British Navy," devote five pages to the *Wellington* incident, and the following is the concluding paragraph:

> We have been tempted to suggest that the War was won by sea power. We were wrong. It was won by sailors—equally of the Merchant Marine as of the Navy. From Coronel to Kiao Chao, from Archangel to Cocus Keeling, no less in Lieutenant D'Oyly Hughes stumbling through a Turkish farm-yard than in Admiral Jellicoe at Whitehall, no less in Lieutenant Brown trying to salve the *Wellington* than in Sir David Beatty directing the Grand Fleet. It was men that triumphed by virtue of the spirit in them and the great traditions that they had inherited—to be handed down in turn as it had been handed down to themselves by Raleigh and Blake, Collingwood and Nelson.

Following this cruise the *Seneca* made a Mediterranean cruise on which an unsuccessful attack occurred on September 30. In this case both the periscope and the torpedo fired were plainly sighted, but the latter missed its mark—the leading vessel on the flank column. The *Seneca*, on the other flank, passed around the stern of the convoy, chased the fleeing periscope, and laid a barrage of depth charges, bringing up a quantity of oil.

Arriving at Gibraltar from this cruise, we were greeted by the sad news of the loss of the cutter *Tampa* with all on board, consisting of her complement of seven officers, four warrant officers, and ninety-eight men of the Coast Guard, and a number of passengers, including three officers and one enlisted man of the United States Navy, one officer and ten seamen of the British Navy, and five British civilians. This occurred just two hours after she had left her convoy in Bristol Channel, under instructions to proceed to Milford Haven, some sixty miles distant, on the evening of September 26, 1918. Information from German sources, information from the listening-in stations on shore in the British Isles, and all the circumstances, showed conclusively that it was through action of an enemy submarine.

The record of the *Tampa* had been a magnificent one. In a special letter to the *Tampa's* commanding officer, Captain Charles Satterlee, dated just three weeks before her loss, Rear Admiral Niblack called attention to the fact that she had escorted eighteen convoys between Gibraltar and the United Kingdom without the loss of a ship; that she was ever ready when called upon, with only one request for repairs, and this for two minor items. It is of interest to note that not a single court-martial, not even a deck court, had been held on board the *Tampa* for her period in the war zone.

The loss of this cutter with so many fine officers and men, following so closely the loss of eleven men from the *Seneca*, and after the majority of the lost had borne so great a part of the heat and burden of the war, naturally produced a profound impression.

A few days later the *Seneca* made her final trip as ocean escort to Milford Haven, on which there occurred another unsuccessful attack, the firing of a torpedo at the convoy by a submarine on October 17, 1918.

Shortly after the return to Gibraltar came the historic date, November 11, 1918, bringing the welcome news of the Armistice, enthusiastically celebrated by a joyful din of whistling, a speech by the governor from his balcony in the evening, and such other celebrations as were feasible.

6

"The Coast Guard in the War"

Lieutenant (jg) Claiborne Pell, USCGR

U.S. Naval Institute *Proceedings*
(December 1942): 1744–46

OVER A YEAR AGO "The Coast Guard as a Naval Asset" appeared in these pages. Since then we have had our declaration of a war which has so far been an essentially naval one for the United States. We have had an ample opportunity to see this asset at work and to permit a brief description of its role in the Navy.

Although many Coast Guard units had been operating directly under Navy orders ever since the declaration of an unlimited National Emergency on May 27, 1941, it was not until November 1, 1941, that the whole service was officially transferred from the jurisdiction of the Secretary of the Treasury to that of the Secretary of the Navy. On that day the vertically striped Treasury commission pennant flying from the truck of all Coast Guard vessels was replaced by the longitudinally striped Navy pennant. However, logistically, the various floating and shore units continued to function according to regular Coast Guard procedure. The present duties of the Coast Guard are of a primarily threefold nature—regular, special war time, and port security.

The regular, peace-time function of the Coast Guard has always been that of a maritime policeman. Like any successful policeman it has discovered that prevention is the best cure. Accordingly it has among its duties the maintenance of lighthouses, lightships, radio beacons, buoys, and all the aids to marine navigation.

Coast Guard cutters on Weather Patrol continuously manned the two weather stations and collected and forwarded meteorological data for the benefit of ocean shipping and the transatlantic clippers. Each spring, when the great bergs from the Greenland Ice Cap started on their way south to eventually melt in the Gulf Stream, Coast Guard cutters on Ice Patrol would search the area, chart the bergs and destroy those that blocked the shipping lanes.

The Greenland and Alaska patrols were likewise preventative and humanitarian in nature in that they brought justice and medical care to the peoples of those northern regions.

Another approach towards preventing casualties at sea was by the education of the mariners. The need for this was shown by an analysis of motorboat assistance reports. Vice Admiral (then Rear Admiral) R. R. Waesche, Commandant of the Coast Guard, said, "We found that from 80 to 90 per cent of those disasters were avoidable. They were either due to faulty equipment, or lack of equipment, or incompetence of the operators."[1] The Coast Guard Reserve Act of 1939 remedied this by checking safety equipment and educating the motorboatmen. In 1941 it was amended by the addition of a military reserve to augment the civilian auxiliary.

The oldest regular Coast Guard duties were its direct revenue activities dating back to the Tariff Act of 1790. Through these it has always been its job to prevent the illegal entry into our country of all contraband-liquors, narcotics, or aliens.

Two hundred and forty surf stations had their men patrolling our shore line equipped with flares and flashlights. When a surfman saw distress signals, he would set off his flares, contact his station, and soon a surfboat would be on its way or a breeches buoy rigged between the unlucky vessel and the beach.

Naturally these regular duties have been vastly altered by war-time conditions. For instance, there is now no such thing as the separate Alaska Patrol, although Coast Guard men and vessels still operate in the Bering Sea. On the other hand the Greenland Patrol has assumed tremendous importance since the service has undertaken the protection of that strategic area with its potential value as an air base and its rich cryolite mines at Ivigtut. Accurate information of weather and the position of the ice floes and bergs is necessary to the success of escort operations, and the responsibility for these factors still rests in part with the Coast Guard even though the former Ice Patrol and Weather Patrol no longer function in the same way or the same locations as in peace time.

There are more than enough opportunities to carry on regular life-saving traditions now that the torpedo has been added to the normal hazards of the sea. Beach patrols are still maintained, but the surf-men are armed in readiness for any more saboteurs that might attempt to land upon our shores. The use of horses has increased the scope of some of these individual patrols.

The special war-time duties of the Coast Guard usually mean direct participation by individual Coast Guard vessels and personnel in Navy task units. For instance, the half dozen cutters of the 327-foot class are assigned to escort duty. These seaworthy vessels are especially useful in heavy weather when taking a tow or on long-legged convoy routes when destroyers and corvettes may eventually be unable to patrol their stations because of lack of fuel. The seagoing cutters of the 165- and 125-foot classes are practically all engaged with the Navy on coastal convoys and antisubmarine patrol. They are aided in this work by Coast Guard aviators who, manning their own and Navy planes, operate from any of the nine Coast Guard air stations.

Some of the troop transports are Coast Guard officered and manned. And the coxswains that guide the landing barges ashore from any transport—whether Army or Navy—are often specially trained Coast

Guardsmen. They have distinguished themselves especially during the landing operations in the Solomon Islands.

Another function was assumed by the Coast Guard when the Bureau of Merchant Marine Navigation and Inspection was consolidated with it by an Executive Order on February 28, 1942. This Bureau, headed by Captain R. S. Field, is responsible for the general safety and protection of all our merchant vessels and their crews. In addition, the War Department has asked this bureau to inspect all transports before leaving the port of embarkation.

The most important single responsibility of the Coast Guard is for the safety from fire, sabotage, or negligence of all water fronts in the United States. This includes inland waterways and the Great Lakes as well as along the coasts. Coast Guard responsibility began on June 27, 1940, when the Espionage Act of 1917 was invoked. This gave certain powers controlling the anchoring and berthing of ships to the Secretary of the Treasury. An amendment has since transferred these powers to the Secretary of the Navy whensoever the Coast Guard operates under the Navy, and the Anchorage Regulations have been issued and amended ever since. However, there was still not enough centralization of authority, so on February 25, 1942, the President issued Executive Order 9074 which gave to the Navy primary responsibility for water-front security. The Secretary of the Navy placed it upon the Coast Guard by his letter of April 29, 1942, to Admiral King and Admiral King's letter of June 13, 1942, to Vice Admiral Waesche.

The Port Security Section at Coast Guard Headquarters was set up to carry out this responsibility. Captain W. N. Derby was its first chief and it now is administered by Captain N. B. Hall. There is a Rear Admiral on each coast who coordinates Port Security activities in the Districts. The District Coast Guard Officer is the supervisory agency while the Captain of the Port is the actual enforcing agent. These new requirements have made tremendous demands upon the Coast Guard's available man power.

This demand is not only for the guarding of the water front from the land side, but the manning of the hundreds of Coast Guard picket and reserve boats that patrol the harbors and of the 250 fire boats for which the Coast Guard has contracted. The training school at Fort McHenry, Baltimore, has helped in training men for this specialized work.

All these new duties have necessitated a huge increase in the size of the Coast Guard. More men are now being shipped in a single month than were in the whole service less than two years ago. All told there are more than 100,000 men wearing the Coast Guard uniform.

The war-time operations of the Coast Guard have not been without their casualties. For instance, to take two geographic poles, the 327-foot cutter *Alexander Hamilton* was torpedoed off Iceland and the transport *Wakefield* was damaged by a direct bomb hit off Singapore. More recently, the *Muskeget* was lost with over a hundred men and without a single clue as to its fate while, in the Solomons, Coast Guardsmen have been killed both in landing operations and on board the *Little, Gregory*, and *McCauley*.

The function of the Coast Guard in the Navy needs, perhaps, some interpretation. It is doing exactly as it did in the last war when it assumed its war-time role as part of the Navy, fought its hardest under it, and suffered the largest percentile loss of life of any of the armed services. The feeling of the service is, as Vice Admiral Waesche said, "We are proud to be a part of the Navy in this war and eager to do well the tasks assigned us."[2] But there is a strong esprit de corps of its very own. It has its own Academy and its own specialized duties. It has a full-time job in peace as well as war. And it has humanitarian traditions of lifesaving, property saving and, through its revenue duties, of money saving that are justly subordinated to its prime mission of today—to destroy the enemy. The Coast Guard is not only proud to be part of the Navy, but is proud of the responsible role assigned to it by the Navy. It is an exemplary unit of democracy, both proud of itself and yet glad to serve.

Notes

1. *Hearings before the Committee on Merchant Marine and Fisheries on H. R. 562.* U.S. Government Printing Office, Washington, 1941. Page 8.

2. "The War Effort of the Coast Guard"—a speech by Vice Admiral Waesche on August 2, 1942, in Boston, Mass.

Pell later became a U.S. Senator from Rhode Island, served on active duty during World War II, and retired from the Coast Guard Reserve in 1978 as a captain.

"Semper Paratus"

7

Lieutenant Commander R. T. Leary, USCGR

U.S. Naval Institute *Proceedings*
(April 1944): 405–14

TUCKED NEATLY AWAY IN THE ARCHIVES of several nations is the history of a battle. A battle which took place on one of those remote and peaceful atolls of the Pacific that the havoc of war had not visited since the Microneseans drove the Polynesians out with their shark-tooth swords many centuries ago. Where the Microneseans still lived in peaceful contentment and watched the coming and going of the Japanese with little concern, where they dug their taro, husked their coconuts, and sailed their canoes on that memorable November 20, 1943.

Marines were swarming in over the reefs of Tarawa. Cruisers, battleships, and destroyers were shelling; dive bombers zoomed down; strafing planes roared overhead. Clouds of smoke and dust rose from an inferno of battle such as the world has seldom seen. More and more Marines came in and fell face down on the reefs, moving always ahead, and from where they died, more drove forward till slowly the inferno ceased and the ships moved in to consolidate.

On board these ships came veterans of many battles, many invasions. To them this was not the story of a battle nor a routine amphibious operation; it was the start of something new and revolutionary, something of which they were to see much more in the months and miles that were to follow, to Tokyo. North Africa had been its own type of invasion, Rendova another, Attu something else, Kiska, Sicily, and on down the list. Each had been a definite campaign and was *pau* (over with). The Gilberts campaign was something new to all of us and it was not to be over so soon. It had in reality just started and those facts that burrowed themselves deep into our minds and souls at Tarawa stand merely as a foundation for those operations which are destined to sweep the Central Pacific. There will be many more Tarawas, Makins, and Apamamas.

Fools and drunkards are blessed by the divine guidance of some deity which keeps them out of harm's way, everyone is blessed by parents or guardians, and yet the invasion commander goes into strange and treacherous waters blessed by no one or nothing except his own cunning, skill, experience, training, and seamanship. These are nothing material or tangible; they are nothing on which one may lean with impunity, they are varying factors, the unknown and the unfathomable. It is sometimes not pleasant, for opposing these elements of success are the cruelly realistic material factors of failure. In dead-reckoning terms, for every knot made through the water, there is a three-knot head current. And should one in command be missing one of the unknown factors in his favor, he increases the head current and may soon consider himself fortunate if he is able to be towed home—some have not been.

It may seem strange that we cannot train and drill men more thoroughly for what they are going to meet in such amphibious operations. They are trained better all the time; yet they are never thoroughly versed in that which may mean life or death to them and those who ride with them. The answer is simple. Sailors are not all products of education. Most of those who are worthy of the name are born, or at least born with that which can be molded into a sailor. America is a seagoing nation; she brings many sailors into the world each year. She failed to step up production in the early years of our century to keep up with our war-time shipbuilding program. Then there are those potential sailors who were lured to the proverbial chicken farm in the hills before they went to sea rather than after they had retired with the marks of untold gales furrowed deeply into their faces. Even a potential sailor takes years and years to perfect. The longer he goes to sea the more he looks back with pride and reassurance on those years which he has spent gaining that assurance and knowledge which is not for the buying at any bookstore.

And so it was when the invasion of North Africa, Rendova, Attu, Kiska, Sicily, and Tarawa took place. Each had its shortcomings, each was better than the last, and each was successful. I wonder who looked after those ships and men. I think it falls to Poseidon and that seagoing nation back east of the 130th meridian.

It was moonlight that morning. The Japs knew we were coming in, had known for weeks. Not the exact day and the hour, but they knew and they were waiting. A lone mine sweeper crept in toward the reef. Somewhere in the moonlight was a pass. There were no buoys, no lights, and the outdated and slightly inaccurate sailing directions for the lagoon stressed the fact that even in broad daylight the beacon, far out in the middle of the lagoon and used for obtaining a bearing on which to enter the lagoon, was hard to see. It blended beautifully into the background of islands on the far side of the lagoon as the reef blended into the breakers and sparkling waves which surrounded it.

At the end of the reef was a sand bar. For this the eager eyes of the mine sweeper's officers looked. They thought they had it. In the moonlight the light blue gave way to the deeper shades of deep water. There was suddenly a rending shock throughout the mine sweeper as her underwater sound apparatus bounced on the reef that was not quite deep enough.

Then the fireworks started. The Japs who had been lying quietly let go with what they could bring to bear. The mine sweeper had found the channel. She sailed into the lagoon. The shells were flying at her hot and heavy. They came in salvos. The first was over, a little too close for comfort. Everybody on deck unconsciously ducked. One short, a straddle, and another. Each time the shells whined overhead, the mine sweeper's crew prayed and ducked. There were seven straddles—no hits. Miraculous but true. The mine sweeper went inside the lagoon, planted a few buoys, turned around, came out, as the moonlight gave way to morning and all hell broke loose from both ships and shore.

One big gun after another on the shore was silenced by the crushing blows of our men-of-war. The ships moved closer, to point-blank range. A battleship's 16-inch guns at 3000 yards is nothing to induce an enemy to stay and fight, yet they stayed. Destroyers moved into the lagoon; others skirted the outside reef. Their fire was accurate and deadly as they picked off gun emplacements, pill boxes, and magazine areas.

At "H" hour the Marines were to go ashore. The transports were close to the reef now and the fire still heavy, but all hands were confident, nobody could live through such a pounding. Down the rope nets on which they had so often practiced invasion tactics went the Marines. Small landing craft waited for them, and like a million beetles crawling over the sparkling surface of the morning sea they pushed their way in through the channel and over the sand bar at the end of the reef into the lagoon. Amtracks, known as Alligators which are nothing more than lightly armored swimming tanks, crawled out of the bows of the LST's, sprawled into the ocean, and swam for the lagoon and the western reef. The larger landing craft were being loaded with tanks and halftracks. The invasion was on.

Under the cover of fire from the Support Force the swarms of infantry-bearing beetles headed for the beach. There were waves of them. The beach was studded with mines, boat traps, mounds of coral, sharp iron stakes. To get the men ashore they had to be crossed. It called for superb seamanship and daring. One by one the boats hung up. The shore opened up in a solid wall of fire. Bullets whined, explosives fell, and boats split asunder like cardboard boxes. Some sank, others grounded and stuck. Marines went off into the water to wade those tortuously long yards to the beach. Those boats that were able to pick up loads of the wounded and return to their ships did so and then they beached again and returned again with more wounded.

The Amtracks swam in. When they beached they crawled and kept on coming, when they fell into bomb craters on the reef they swam and still kept coming. Always they came and the shells ripped through them. They crawled ashore, behind the Jap lines they crawled, and hand grenades were thrown into the Jap fire pits from behind. The Marines had landed.

The LCM's now came ashore with their tanks. They also crawled up behind the lines and overran the island. One coxswain landed his tank, put his engines full astern, retracted, turned, and sped for the open sea again for another tank. As he cleared his last navigational obstacle, he turned to look where he had landed his tank. She was still there. She was split wide open, burning, smoking, and broken. He jammed his throttles down, sped out to the transports and cargo ships, came back with another tank.

For the dozens of Amtracks that reached the shore as many more dozens lay wrecked on the reef and beach.

More than men, now were wanted equipment, food, water, medicine, doctors, and most dearly of all fuel for the flamethrowers that were to work night and day during the days that followed. The LCM's, LCVP's, ship's boats, and craft of all descriptions were turned to the carrying of precious necessities to push the beachhead which had been gained to its ultimate success. LST's that had launched Alligators rolled slightly over on their sides and launched 108-foot LCT's from their decks. They too joined in the carrying of cargo. Slow and arduously the necessary items came ashore.

And as the small boats cleared from the reef, the guns, trucks, and heavy equipment came crawling in over the reef as the tide ebbed and left a dry boulevard to the shore. At the edge of the reef, with their jaws yawning wide and their ramps down were the LST's. No boats were needed to unload them, they sailed to surrounding reef, stuck their bows up on the coral, and discharged their cargoes. Some cargo went ashore by its own locomotion, other by the use of trucks which backed aboard and came out piled as from a warehouse. When their bellies were unloaded a great elevator as on an aircraft carrier lifted trucks, jeeps, and trailers, drums of oil and gasoline, and other bits of cargo from the decks of these shore-ramming cargo ships and that gear also rolled out of their bows and ran across the reef to the shore.

Japs watched from fox holes, pill boxes, blockhouses, fire pits, and gun emplacements. They lost their nerve and dug deeper, refused to come out. They lost face, lost battles, and lost their lives, for that which had taken them two years to land, the Americans were landing in two days. What they had done with coolie labor we did with bottled horses, the equipment swept ashore.

They had spent two years digging into emplacements which they were dug out of in three days. A few more days and the Wildcat fighters were settling down on the field which the Seabees had quickly renovated. Beside them sat Jap "Bettys" and "Zeros" which would sting no more. And rapidly the two square miles of island changed from a battlefield to a construction project. Jap trucks and steam rollers were put to work and hundreds of American trucks came to join them. The machines buzzed day and night, and though Japs sniped and land mines blew up, and planes bombed, the work went on unimpeded. Where one man fell, five more took his place.

A lone Seabee started in across the reef with his tractor. In tow he had a bundle of pipes which he had picked up from a boat at the reef's edge. The area of reef which he had to cross had not been checked for land mines. He did not like the looks of it. Guided by some instinct he headed his tractor for an opening in the tank traps on the reef, dismounted, and went back to ride on the pipes as his tractor crawled slowly ashore. Between the tank traps there was a tremendous explosion. The tractor flew 30 feet into the air, came down as nuts and bolts. Out from under the load of pipes jumped the cautious Seabee. Ashore came the Seabee to get another tractor. He was cursing under his breath; ". . . Damn," he said, "fell down on the coral and scratched myself." He licked the back of his hand and went back to get the pipe.

The small landing craft kept up a continual shuttle from the transports and freighters to the beach. Their loads were small and much of them had to be unloaded at the coconut pier which the Japs had left for us. This was not satisfactory, however, and as quickly as the LST's discharged their initial cargoes they went alongside freighters, opened great hatches in their decks and filled up their spacious tank decks and main decks with cargo that was delivered en masse directly to the beach.

Not only had one of the greatest battles of history just taken place, but now one of the greatest engineering masterpieces of the war was becoming a reality. The Gilberts were not the objective, they were merely the steppingstone. Before we could step farther, airfields, gun emplacements, and camps had to be built. Before the smoke had cleared, the Seabees were at work putting in a second airfield up the lagoon half again as big as the one which they already had at Betio. Our heavy fighters went through the thin coral and cement surface of the Betio field, and a few of them spun in. The Seabees calmly set about resurfacing it. While medium bombers and fighters raided the Marshalls the Seabees surfaced half of the field with their own formula which was scooped up off the reef and dumped on the airfield. And while planes used the new half they resurfaced the old.

Yes, it was as simple as that; there was a job to be done, they did it. But beyond the astonishing manner in which things seemed to happen was the omnipresent fact that things were in reality, as we call them, FUBAR. That is similar to SNAFU, as we used to say in Iceland, but it all means the same thing and always will, just as invasions will, due to their very nature, always be one or the other.

There were bound to be difficulties and drawbacks and they were indeed plentiful in this particular lagoon. I have mentioned the lone mine sweeper that ventured in, swept the channel, planted her buoys and returned safely out to sea again. The conditions under which she operated were indeed bad. But hundreds of ships and smaller craft followed her, and even in broad daylight things were not good.

Unlike many, or I should say most South and Central Pacific lagoons, Tarawa has a murky one. Some times it is fairly clear and visibility into the water is good. It is an old practice in these islands to do one's piloting by the natural chart, which vision of the bottom affords you, rather than bother with running ranges and taking bearings and using lead lines, etc. By knowing your colors and coral you can neatly pilot a ship through any lagoon where there is good visibility providing there is enough water there to float your ship. In some lagoons you dodge the dark-colored water and in others you dodge the light, though in most cases, if it is normally clear, you can see exactly what lies 4 or 5 fathoms below you.

Tarawa lagoon is the exception and ships for years have been somewhat skeptical of the place. For some reason the water seems to have a tendency to keep bits of coral suspended in it which make it slightly milky. When a ship's screws churn up the water of this lagoon they leave a milky mess which also helps to obliterate the bottom. Some days it is not so bad and then on others you can barely see the edge of the fringing reef which is very prominent indeed. It is not recommended that more than six ships anchor in the lagoon at once as there are known to be coral heads in various areas which make navigation treacherous. The Japs never had more than two in there according to an old native sailor friend I ran into at Eita village. He said, "Two come. They go, two more come. Never more than two."

So it was that the Japs had answered the problem of the murky lagoon and the coral heads. Three days after we took the place we had many more than two ships in the harbor. They were ocean-going ships of all varieties from man-of-war on down.

How was it done? We really can't say, but it was, and there were at the time no casualties from coral heads. Astounding and hair-raising discoveries were made from time to time throughout the harbor, and these were promptly marked with buoys till we felt that we could proceed about the harbor even in the murky water with some degree of safety. Then came the sound boats and with them more amazing discoveries and we too began to wonder how it had been done.

There was one particularly bad shoal nearly in the middle of the harbor. One of the sound boats proceeding in deep water suddenly got a 2½-fathom reading on it. The next sounding was deep again. It was a small shoal, but a treacherous one. The next day a diver was sent down. Around and around he wandered looking for that shoal, but nowhere could he find it. That had happened before, so he continued to look. Finally he emerged. Beneath his helmet was a broad grin. "That shoal," he said, "is one of our own tank lighters standing neatly on its transom, bow up."

Others were real, and as our forces began to branch out to the other islands some of the real ones began to be discovered in a realistic fashion. Every day or so someone would turn up with a wilted screw or a damaged rudder. Some turned up with holes in their tanks. But as we go on to the more serious of the casualties we must first survey the reefs on which they landed, for by far the highest casualties were in landing craft.

One beach which the larger craft frequented was of a fairly good variety. It was necessary to hook the bow of the ship up on a reef but the sterns for the most part stayed afloat. Usually in landing you could slide in between the coral heads so that when the tide went out the ugly heads did not stick up through your engine-room. If the tide was too high when you rammed into the reef you slid up on top of it and when the tide went out you were nearly high and dry. If the tide was too low when you beached you simply bumped, buckled in the middle and bit, and stayed where you were with your engines going ahead.

Even though you have a 3,000-pound Danforth anchor astern to hold you, if your bow is not solid on the reef you slide off at high water. This is unpleasant for several reasons.

As the ships must get slightly up on the edge of the reef, they must come in at high water. The reef on which they beach is usually 500 or 600 yards across. It is nearly level. Therefore, for at least half of the day it is covered with the high water as when the ship beached. As the tide ebbs, a bulldozer comes rushing out and scooping up the coral on either side of the ship's bow builds a coral ramp on which the vehicles may come and go even at half tide. This speeds up unloading considerably. But should the ship slide at high water and float away from the coral ramp, you have the distasteful job of trying to retract and hit the exact same spot. With a 5,500-ton ship that handles as if she were related to a crab this is not often an easy thing to do with a beam wind. There were often enough wrecked Amtracks on the reef so that we could secure our bows to them. When not, we drove stakes and chained our ramps to them. It was like tying up a horse, for they pranced and wiggled around very unmannerly on the high water.

But all the beaches were not as easy as this one which we were fortunate enough to go to first. Farther up the lagoon were those beaches where you slid in and invariably half or two-thirds of your ship would be hung up at low water. These beaches were also lavishly fringed with coral heads with just the right amount of water over them at slack flood so that you slid in on them and then rested. It was best to put on a diving mask and take a swim under your ship when you beached in such places. There was one advantage to the presence of the coral heads. If you could manage to slide the ship over against one you would be certain that she was going to go nowhere with the wind.

The first day that I ever went aboard an LST I was certain that they were the weirdest ships afloat. The weirdest had not come, nor do I think it has yet come, for as we charge around these lagoons beaching, loading, unloading, transferring, sailing all over the Pacific, we are always running into something absurd to the seaman and yet so practical to the needs of the LST skipper. "Slide your ship up against a coral head, mate, and you'll be certain she won't go anywhere with the wind."

If I'd made that statement two years ago I would have been ushered off to a seaman's rest home for recuperation. Yet how wonderfully some of these anti-seagoing bits of seamanship work out. Perhaps it is often the better of two evils that makes them so because if you are sitting up against a coral head you are not sitting on it, which really raised hob. If you do bounce off a coral head or land on the top of a pile of the things and get well perforated you have made what we call a "Pearl Harbor beaching."

As you go on up the lagoon you come across an LCM aground or one of the other small landing craft hung up on the reef. They ferry the equipment from the harbor up to the remote corners of the islands where sand bars, reefs, and coral heads make the going treacherous and nearly impossible. But for those who have been on the LST's since their late arrival in this war there seems to be nothing beyond the ability of these ships that can load anywhere, carry anything, and dump it off anywhere again with little effort and great speed.

Unloading was going slowly at our reef-fringed, tide-swept coral boulevard. The Air Corps wanted the cargo desperately, and they were getting it desperately slow. Up and down astern of us roared the small boats, pontoon barges, and landing craft. They were proceeding up to the coral quay which had been built for them to unload at. It was deep enough off the quay so that they came and went at all tides; they were never still. The Army captain in charge of the cargo in the hold looked with longing eyes up the lagoon, for there too was where his cargo was supposed to go. Everyone knew that the lagoon was impassable beyond where we sat among our coral heads. This was the farthest a ship had ever gone. "If we could only get up to that coral quay," groaned the Army captain.

"Maybe we can," I said, and the Army officer looked at me with a mixture of alarm, sympathy, skepticism, and doubt. He had been reading the *Coast Guard Magazine* on his trip up from the Ellice Group and he had a certain amount of respect for what that branch of the service stood for and did, but his conclusion on my latest statement was that we had either been in the tropics too long or that we were getting war happy.

It was certainly neither, for with that same satisfaction that comes out of being a part of the outfit that is revolutionizing amphibious warfare we put out in one of our landing craft to see just what things looked like in the upper lagoon. It was the first time I'd heaved a lead line since I left the *Yankee* and I felt as if I were back on the deck of that venerable craft. There was nothing she couldn't do, and somehow it seemed at that moment that this job could be done also.

We were half an hour getting to the end of that coral dock, and it was getting dark. We took soundings as fast as we could in the growing dusk, and then suddenly, as it does in the tropics, night closed in upon us.

One thing I had found out. There was water off the dock—also two big coral patches and a sand bar. But there was still water, and where there is water a ship can go.

On our way up we had followed the deep water with our eyes as best we could and we were certain that there was a pass through the two reefs which cut that section of the lagoon in two.

Going back we bounced on a shoal. There was a moon coming up and we could begin to see the reefs we bounced on, so we could go to starboard, bounce, grate, and slide over, then bounce again. The tide was falling. All around us now were reefs and it seemed that we might be stuck, to spend the night poking blindly around in the lagoon trying to get through the reefs. Then under the edge of the moon appeared a dark ribbon of water. There really was a pass through the reef and we roared through it. Now and again we heaved the lead—"good water."

The next morning when the tide and the sun were both high, a lone LST slid out from among the coral heads and headed up the lagoon in a direction in which ships had never gone before. Her small boat followed along behind her like a patient dog as she crept slowly ahead weaving and dodging the light patches in the water. From the flying bridge the dark ribbon of water soon showed through the reefs. Into this the 69 stuck her 50 feet of beam. Her bow slid over the coral as her stern swung around into the deep water, and on she went.

On the coral dock work temporarily stopped, for the big ship was getting close now. She squeezed and wormed but the leadsman sang back his soundings. Four hundred yards off the dock a boat came hurriedly alongside with a confused CPO in it. We couldn't land there, couldn't get in, but the bow of the ship was pointed and she still crept ahead. With the last sand bar swinging under her stern she slid diagonally toward the end of the quay. On she went and the people on the quay moved back. Beside her now were the pontoon floats at the end of the quay. Her bow slid up over the sand, slid on a few yards until it climbed a foot or so up the sloping coral and sand side of the quay and stopped. The doors swung open and the ramp eased down onto a dry road and the best unloading platform yet.

Of all the places that the LST's have found to beach, this was the seaman's dream. The tide did not matter. The ballast tanks were flooded and she sat firmly where her bow had slid up over the sand, and the wind did not bother her. Trucks came and went 24 hours a day.

A Japanese officer was brought aboard one of our cruisers for questioning. He was alive, he was too bewildered to commit hara-kiri. Educated in our own colleges he spoke fluent English. What did he have to say?

"It can't have fallen, it couldn't be taken in four days. It would take a million men six months to capture Tarawa." He was bewildered.

We're sorry, mate; we had neither the million men nor the six months to waste on Tarawa. It *is* taken—that is all you need to know. Your first impregnable line of defense, that line that could stand six months against a million men without the support of your fleet or your air power has fallen. We have an invitation to accept also, mate.

Just off the beach so appropriately designated as Red Beach lies a wreck. The wreck of a small Jap coastal steamer. The first day of the invasion of Tarawa it was a harmless rusty mass of iron. The next day one of our landing craft left the beach with a load of casualties to go back out to the transports. It passed close by this wreck as it made for the pass in the reef. From the wreck came a plaintive call, "Hey, Marine, how's to give us a lift, we're stranded?"

"Sorry, Mac," came back the Marine guard in the boat, "got a load of wounded aboard I've got to get out right away." At those words and with the boat drawing away fast the spokesman opened fire with a machine gun.

"So you're stranded are you? Well, just sit tight, Mac, we'll be along to pick you up and all your brothers too, till we have you all safely stowed away back on Honshu."

Lieutenant Commander Leary commanded a Coast Guard manned LST in the invasion of Tarawa, and in this article he explains many of the details of the landing that have hitherto been lacking. Of equal importance he points out the particular difficulties of landing craft in attacking the reef-encircled coral atolls of the Pacific.

"A Mission of Higher Classification"

8

Richard Russell

U.S. Naval Institute *Proceedings*
(August 2005): 26–27

In the waning months of World War II, U.S. Sailors and Coast Guardsmen trained Soviet naval personnel in the handling of vessels scheduled for transfer to the Soviet Pacific Ocean Fleet for use in the climactic fight against Japan. When the war ended abruptly, the special deal proved to be less than the bargain that it first seemed.

WHEN THE U.S. DECLARED WAR on the Axis powers following the devastating attack on Pearl Harbor on 7 December 1941, President Franklin D. Roosevelt asked the Soviet Union to enter the war against Japan. Instead, Stalin and his USSR steadfastly remained neutral. Finally, in October 1944, with Hitler's Third Reich doomed to defeat, Stalin acquiesced to American requests and set the price for Soviet involvement in the war against Japan. He stipulated that the Allies must establish a reserve of supplies and equipment in the Soviet Far East and endorse the Soviet Union's territorial claims in East Asia. These included transfer of the Kuril Islands to Soviet control and acknowledging what amounted to U.S. and Soviet spheres of influence in northern China, Manchuria, and Korea. At the February 1945 Yalta Conference, President Roosevelt secured Stalin's promise to enter the war two to three months after the defeat of Germany by accepting these terms.

American planners wasted little time in creating a special project (code-named Milepost) to stockpile the requested war materiel. Milepost had a large naval component, known as Project Hula, which comprised not only a substantial Soviet shopping list of aircraft and equipment, but also 250 naval vessels. The vessels would augment existing Soviet naval units and support amphibious operations against Japanese outposts on Sakhalin and in the Kuril Islands.

To help Soviet officers and men make the best use of their warships, the U.S. Navy established a special unit (Navy Detachment 3294) of Navy and Coast Guard personnel to train some 15,000 Soviet sailors and transfer 180 of these vessels to Soviet custody by 1 November 1945, the original target date for the invasion of Kyushu (Operation Olympic). Based at Cold Bay, at the extreme tip of the Alaskan Peninsula, the secret operation was designated Hula-2. Captain William S. Maxwell, U.S. Navy, was in command. Commander John J. Hutson, U.S. Coast Guard, was his deputy and training officer. The Coast Guard presence at Cold Bay was considerable, because of the presence of the frigate crews. This entire vessel type, throughout the Navy, was crewed exclusively by Coast Guard officers and men.

Beginning on 10 April 1945, a Soviet merchant ship carrying 500 men arrived at Cold Bay each day for five days, launching the program. Rear Admiral Boris D. Popov, commander of the 5th Independent Detachment of Soviet Navy Ships, the official unit designation of the Soviet naval contingent at Cold Bay, arrived on 11 April. Captain Maxwell attributed Project Hula's success, in part, to Admiral Popov's cooperative attitude.

Training began immediately. Despite miserable weather, a lack of Russian linguists, and eager but woefully unprepared Soviet trainees, the

Russian sailors mastered their tasks, first in a shore-based training program, and eventually in their vessels. Some of the more outstanding personnel became instructors themselves. The Soviet navy men lacked experience in radar and sonar technology, but were good engineers and proficient gunners.

Minor delays occurred because of equipment shortages on board the transfer vessels, inadequate training materials, and damage done to the vessels, often the lightly constructed subchasers, but the Soviet-American team kept to a tight schedule. The May and June departures of convoys leaving for Petropavlovsk on Kamchatka comprised landing craft and large minesweepers. Prior to Soviet entry into the war on 9 August, the Soviet navy had received 100 vessels: 10 frigates (PF), 30 landing craft (LCI(L)), 18 large minesweepers (AM), 19 wooden-hulled minesweepers (YMS), 20 subchasers (SC), and three floating repair shops (YR).

Until ordered by Fleet Admiral Ernest J. King, the U.S. Chief of Naval Operations and Commander-in-Chief U.S. Fleet, on 5 September, to cease transfers, crews hoisted the Soviet naval ensign over another 49 vessels: 18 frigates, 6 large minesweepers, 12 wooden-hulled minesweepers, 18 subchasers, and one floating repair shop. Of note, the U.S. crew of USS *Hoquiam* (PF-5), transferred in August, included African-American Coast Guardsmen. In total, Navy Detachment 3294 had trained some 12,000 Soviet officers and men, including at least one future admiral. The last of the Soviet-manned vessels, a frigate, didn't depart Cold Bay until 17 September.

The atomic attacks, combined with the Red Army's multi-pronged attack on Japanese forces in Manchuria and Korea, starting on 9 August, brought the war in Asia and the Pacific to an abrupt end, precluding a costly U.S.-led invasion of the Japanese home islands. Anglo-American offensive operations halted on 15 August, but fighting between Soviet and Japanese forces continued.

The American-Soviet political relationship had deteriorated since the spring. With Roosevelt's death on 12 April 1945, new president Harry S. Truman inherited a variety of contentious political issues connected to postwar Europe. The successful test of the atomic bomb in July 1945 (and the diplomatic advantages it offered) led the Truman administration to reconsider the desirability of wide-scale Soviet participation in the war, particularly if it meant Soviet involvement in the administration of postwar Japan.

Soviet forces—in some cases, hastily—organized attack and occupation forces, so that their territorial ambitions would not be denied. Vessels obtained at Cold Bay were in the thick of the action, as Soviet naval forces supported ground operations against enemy positions on southern Sakhalin Island (11 August), northern Korea (12 August), and in the Kuril Islands (17 August). While tens of thousands of Japanese surrendered to the Red Army in Manchuria, Japanese defenders at these maritime centers fought tenaciously, giving the Russians a taste of what U.S. Marines and soldiers had experienced during the island campaigns.

The Kuril Islands represented the major objective. On 15 August, Marshall A. M. Vasilevsky, commander-in-chief in the Soviet Far East, ordered the commander of the Kamchatka Defense Zone—flying his flag in *T-334* (Hula's ex-USS *Augury* [AM-149])—to begin the occupation of the chain immediately, starting with an assault on Shumshu, the northernmost island, on 17 August. The ubiquitous LCI(L)s made the occupation possible, but five were lost during the attack, victims of shore batteries. The frigates and large minesweepers, with a main battery of three-inch guns, proved inadequate in the role of gunfire support. Nevertheless, one by one, the islands fell. Stalin considered a Soviet occupation of Hokkaido, but ordered such preparations halted on 22 August. Fighting in the Kuril archipelago ended the next day.

Project Hula satisfied President Roosevelt's enduring objective to link U.S. and Soviet military interests in the North Pacific in opposition to Japan. Yet, even while the last frigates got up steam to depart Cold Bay, Soviet fighters fired on a Navy PBM Mariner seaplane that had flown into restricted airspace over Port Arthur, offering a symbolic end to wartime collaboration. As Soviet-American tensions worsened, Project Hula slipped into obscurity, a footnote to Roosevelt's diplomatic and political legacy. Still, it had a major impact on individual lives, as participants on both sides would later suffer during the Cold War for having once embraced a former ally in cooperation. Even more significant, the Soviet Union and Japan never signed a peace treaty, given the dispute over the "northern territories" (four small islands off Hokkaido that Soviet naval forces equipped with U.S. lend-lease vessels seized in August 1945). Regardless of post-war events, however, Project Hula remains an unparalleled example of wartime allied cooperation.

Richard Russell is associate publisher at Potomac Books, Inc. (formerly Brassey's, Inc.) and the author of *Project Hula: Secret Soviet-American Cooperation in the War Against Japan* (1997), from which this article was derived. From 1989–1999, he was a historian in the Contemporary History Branch of the Naval Historical Center.

9 "Cutters and Sampans"

Senior Chief Dennis L. Noble, USCG (Ret.)

U.S. Naval Institute *Proceedings*
(June 1984): 47–53

ON 10 MAY 1966, *the* USCGC Point Grey *(WPB-82324) was patrolling the east side of Ca Mau Peninsula when her crew spotted bonfires on the beach. While investigating the fires, the patrol boat picked up a steel-hulled target on her radar about six miles to seaward attempting to close the beach. The contact was tentatively identified as a 100-foot Chinese Nationalist vessel, traveling on a course of 260° at ten knots.*[1]

The Point Grey *began to shadow the trawler. At 0240, the trawler was within one mile of the beach opposite the fires, with three to four persons observed on deck. By 0500, the contact was within one-half mile of the beach, and the* Point Grey's *commanding officer notified his operational commander on the destroyer escort USS* Brister *(DER-327) that he would board the trawler at daylight.*

At 0700, the Point Grey *closed the trawler. The craft was found aground and deserted. As the men of the* Point Grey *attempted to board the trawler, they came under fire from the beach. The cutter moved out of small arms range and began to lob 81-mm. mortar rounds at the gun positions on the beach.*

For the next six hours, the Point Grey *kept the trawler under surveillance. At 1330, without air or naval gunfire support, the* Point Grey *again closed the trawler. At about 200 yards from the beach and within 100 yards of the trawler, the cutter came under "extremely" accurate small arms and automatic weapons fire.[2] Within 20 to 30 seconds, three of the four men on the bow of the* Point Grey *were hit: a coastguardsman, a U.S. Army major "along for the ride," and the South Vietnamese Navy liaison officer. Commissaryman Second Class Kepler was the first coastguardsman wounded in the Vietnam War.*

The cutter took about 25 hits, but no one was seriously hurt. Air strikes were called in to suppress the fire. The Point Grey's *crew then boarded the vessel.*

The haul from the trawler proved impressive. Contraband, including an estimated 50–60 tons of arms, ammunition, and supplies, was confiscated.

At 0100 on 14 March 1967, a patrol aircraft spotted a trawler 40 miles offshore and closing the beach. The Brister *began to track the contact by radar and assigned a fast patrol boat, PCF-78, to intercept.*

At 0530, PCF-78 reported that she was under heavy small arms and possible recoilless rifle fire, with many hits and one minor casualty. The USCGC Point Ellis *(WPB-82330) proceeded at high speed to assist.[3] She arrived at 0625 to find that the trawler had been beached.*

The Point Ellis *joined with the* Brister *in shelling the beach. While engaged in the gunfire mission, the commanding officer of the* Point Ellis, *Lieutenant (junior grade) Helton, maneuvered his cutter in a zigzag attack on the trawler. Suddenly, an explosion thundered across the water, and the trawler disappeared in a cloud of smoke. When the smoke cleared, only debris remained.*

Later, salvage operations recovered approximately 1,200 rifles, several machine guns, and miscellaneous ammunition. The Coast Guard War Diary *notes that "amazingly enough," no hits were taken by the* Point Ellis, *probably "attributable to the excellent manner" in which Helton handled his command.*

On 29 April 1965, newspaper readers were surprised to learn that units of the U.S. Coast Guard had been ordered to Vietnam. The U.S. Navy, the newspapers announced, had requested Coast Guard assistance in the form of 82-foot patrol boats. The deployment of these boats marks the beginning of the Coast Guard's role in the Vietnam War.

The Viet Cong were commonly perceived as elusive, silent figures, slipping through the night, living off the land, and, at battle time, mysteriously appearing with weapons cached in a hut or some other hiding place. True, the Viet Cong could live off the land, but they did need a supply line to obtain weapons, ammunition, and other material. The most direct route was the sea.[4]

In 1964, as insurgency increased, the North Vietnamese leaders in Hanoi made an important decision concerning the supply of forces in the south. Until this time, the insurgents had used French, British, and U.S. weapons. Under the new strategy, all arms would be standard, using the same caliber of ammunition, and more modern artillery would be employed. The most important weapon was the AK-47 Soviet assault rifle. Other new weapons included 7.62-mm. machine guns, rocket launchers (RPG-2s), 82mm. Soviet and Chinese mortars, and 47- and 75-mm. recoilless rifles. This required an increase in infiltration.[5] The South Vietnamese Navy was pushed to the limit in trying to patrol 1,200 miles of coastline.

At 1030 on 16 February 1965, Lieutenant James S. Bowers, U.S. Army, flying a helicopter from Qui Nhon, sighted a camouflaged vessel in Vung Ro Bay on the central coast. Bowers radioed Second Coastal Zone Senior Adviser Lieutenant Commander Harvey P. Rogers, U.S. Navy, in Nha Trang.

The vessel, found carrying a large supply of arms and equipment, was engaged and sunk by the Navy. At last, U.S. advisers had proof of infiltration. More important, buried materiel was found nearby, proving that shipments had been increased.[6] The "Vung Ro Incident" led directly to Operation Market Time and the involvement of the U.S. Coast Guard's 82-foot patrol boats in Vietnam.[7]

On 3 March 1965, at the request of General William C. Westmoreland, a conference was held in South Vietnam to discuss seaborne infiltration. Those attending the conference decided that the "best tactic to interdict coastal traffic would be to assist and inspire the Vietnamese Navy to increase the quality and quantity of its searches."[8]

Infiltration of weapons and equipment by sea was accomplished in two ways: by coastwise junk traffic mingling with the more than 50,000 registered civilian craft plying Vietnam's coastal waters; and by vessels of trawler size (usually steel-hulled), which sailed innocently in international waters and, at a given location, would make a perpendicular approach to the coast. The trawlers probably originated in North Vietnam and the People's Republic of China.

To stop trawler infiltration, the conference members proposed that a conventional sea patrol be established by U.S. Navy ships and aircraft. They planned to establish a defensive area extending 40 miles to sea then have South Vietnam authorize U.S. naval forces to stop, board, and search vessels in its waters and the contiguous zone.

The Joint Chiefs of Staff approved the plan on 16 March. On 11 May, the South Vietnamese Government granted permission for Market Time units "to stop, search, and seize vessels not clearly engaged in innocent passage inside the three-mile limit of the Republic of Vietnam's territorial waters."[9] Operation Market Time was now under way.

Market Time operations were divided into nine patrol areas, stretching from the 17th parallel to the Brevie Line in the Gulf of Thailand.[10] Normally, a destroyer escort (radar) or an oceangoing minesweeper was responsible for each patrol area. Five coastal surveillance centers, Da Nang, Qui Nhon, Nha Trang, Vung Tau, and An Thoi, were responsible for coordinating patrol units.[11]

On 16 April 1965, with Market Time planning in full swing, Secretary of the Navy Paul Nitze requested Secretary of the Treasury Henry H. Fowler to inform him on the availability of U.S. Coast Guard units to deploy to Vietnam. Three days later, the Commandant of the Coast

Guard informed the Navy Department that 82-foot and 40-foot patrol boats were available. After a meeting between Navy and Coast Guard officials, the Coast Guard agreed to deploy 17 82-foot patrol boats. The official joint memorandum to the President was sent on 29 April, advising him of the deployment. The next day, U.S. Coast Guard Squadron One was formed.[12]

The patrol boat was ideal for Market Time. She had unique design features that allowed for a small peacetime complement of eight men. The machinery was designed to facilitate underway operations without a continuous engine room watch. Engine speed was controlled by throttles on the bridge. Main engine and generator alarms were also mounted in the wheelhouse. The bridge was designed so that all navigation equipment, radio, radar, and engine controls were centered on a console about the wheel. If necessary, one man could steer, control the speed, guard the radar, observe the Fathometer, and operate the radio. This ability was especially useful when most of the crew was on deck during operations.

The patrol boat was twin-screwed, propelled by two turbo-charged, 600-shaft horsepower VT-12M Cummings diesel engines, one on each shaft. The hull was constructed of black steel and had six water-tight compartments. The superstructure was built of aluminum. The patrol boat displaced 65 tons and, most important, drew only six feet of water.

Finally, she could berth and mess a crew for a short period of time. This craft was the only shallow-water patrol boat that had this ability, thus, she could remain on patrol for longer periods of time.

The patrol boats were modified for their combat role. A 50-caliber machine gun was mounted on top of an 81-mm. mortar. This piggyback armament was then placed on the boat's bow. Four additional 50-caliber machine guns were installed on the main deck, aft the wheelhouse. Ready service boxes were installed on deck to store the additional ammunition. Other changes ranged from better reefers to more bunks.

On 6 May 1965, the 17 patrol boats were loaded as deck cargo on merchant ships in New York, Norfolk, New Orleans, Galveston, San

Pedro, San Francisco, and Seattle. Five days later, coastguardsmen began to report to the West Coast for training.

Initially, 47 officers and 198 enlisted men formed Coast Guard Squadron One. Their four weeks of training consisted of courses in gunnery, communications, escape and evasion, and other military training. After training, the men joined their patrol boats in Subic Bay.

At Subic Bay, the patrol boats received last-minute modifications, crews were assigned, and the squadron was organized. It was divided into two divisions. Division Eleven consisted of eight boats; Division Twelve received the remainder. Division Twelve sailed for Da Nang on 15 July, arriving five days later. Division Eleven sailed on 20 July and arrived at An Thoi on 31 July.[13]

The cutters, as were all Market Time surface units, were expected to "conduct surveillance, gunfire support, visit and search, and other operations as directed along the coast of the Republic of Vietnam in order to assist the Republic of Vietnam in detection and prevention of Communist infiltration from the seas."[14] Because of the many junks, sampans, and other craft in the area, a priority system of boarding had to be established. A ranking of boardings was developed with the following scheme: vessels transiting the area, junks fishing or operating in restricted areas, fishing boats anchored and not working nets, and last, fishing boats working nets.[15]

When ready for patrol, a cutter would report to the minesweeper or destroyer escort maintaining outer barrier patrol. The outer patrol would provide radar and navigational assistance to the cutter. In a like manner, the cutter would provide the same information to South Vietnamese Navy junk units working close to the beach. In the Gulf of Thailand, six of the nine patrol boats were constantly on patrol, each in one of six designated subareas. The boats were under way for four days, and then they returned to the support ship for two days. Each boat rotated through all the subareas.[16]

Life on board the small patrol boats was rough. The crews usually worked from 12 to 16 hours a day when under way. In the Gulf of Thailand area, for instance, the boats had a three-section watch: three men—the officer-of-the-deck, helmsman, and radioman—stood a four-hour watch; a second section served as boarding party; and a third would be off duty. The captain and cook stood no watches. An officer was on hand for all boardings. The men had to be on guard constantly. Any common fishing craft could suddenly open fire with automatic weapons. Eventually, most crew members learned the maxim: "Don't relax. It could mean your life!"[17]

On her first patrol near the 17th parallel, the USCGC *Point Orient* (WPB-82319) came under mortar and machine gun fire. In an incredible oversight, the cutter was still painted her peacetime color of white. As one officer said, "White cutters are a beautiful sight on a moonlit or flarelit night, that is, unless you are on the cutter."[18] The next day, the boats began to be repainted.

When not under way, the patrol boats moored alongside a support ship. While lying to, the coastguardsmen painted, repaired, and took on supplies for the next patrol. The sailors had little time to relax. Moreover, there were no recreational facilities in the boats. Therefore, the Commander, Squadron One, had two spare boat crews so that each man could have five days of rest and recreation every three months.[19]

One Market Time operational policy did not sit well with many coastguardsmen. The Navy's Swift boats were not suited for offshore work in adverse weather. The Coast Guard patrol boats, however, could weather many storms. In September 1967, the Market Time Commander decided that the Coast Guard boats should shift with the seasons. In other words, Coast Guard patrol boats followed the monsoons, while the Navy Swifts followed the sunshine.[20]

In the first month of patrols, the cutter crews boarded more than 1,100 junks and sampans, inspected more than 4,000 Vietnamese craft, and worked more than 4,800 man-hours. To counter the cutters' efforts, the Viet Cong told local fishermen that the U.S. boats were driving them from the best fishing grounds so that U.S. fishing boats could fish there. Indeed, this must have appeared true, for the best fishing grounds were frequently in restricted waters, and the cutters had to displace the fishermen. To counter this move by the Viet Cong, the U.S. Coast Guard, Navy, and South Vietnamese developed a program to help the fishermen, which included medical care.

By October 1965, it became apparent that Market Time forces were spread too thin, especially along Vietnam's southeast coast. On 29 October 1965, Secretary of the Navy Nitze requested an additional nine cutters be deployed to Vietnam. This group, Division Thirteen, took station at Vung Tau in early 1966.[21]

The year was a busy and dangerous one for the men of the small cutters. The USCGC *Point White* (WPB-82308), only in-country for a month, was patrolling in the Soi Rap River area. The cutter's customary operations method was to steam into her area "to show the flag," steam out, and then try to covertly reenter the area. On this occasion, the ruse worked, for the cutter spotted a junk crossing the river and attempted to halt the craft. The junk opened fire with automatic weapons and small arms. The *Point White* returned fire and rammed the junk, throwing the hostile vessel's crew into the water. One of the junk's passengers was a key Viet Cong leader of the Rung Sat Zone.

But junks and sampans were not the only craft firing on the cutters. On the night of 11 August 1966, the USCGC *Point Welcome* (WPB-82329) steamed near the demilitarized zone.[22] Suddenly, the cutter was illuminated and under attack by friendly aircraft. Several hits ripped into the wheelhouse. A gasoline fire blazed on deck. The crew tried to fight the fire and repel the attack simultaneously. Finally, there was nothing to do but run the cutter aground and abandon her.

Later, other Coast Guard units arrived on scene to assist the *Point Welcome*. The rescue units found the commanding officer of the cutter and one crew member dead. The executive officer, two other crewmen, the South Vietnamese liaison officer, and a *Life* magazine reporter were wounded. The *Point Welcome* was refloated and towed to port for repairs.

At the beginning of Operation Market Time, the Chief of the Naval Advisory Group, Rear Admiral Norvell G. Ward, foresaw the necessity of returning the responsibility of naval operations to the South Vietnamese Navy. His command and control decisions were therefore predicated upon training South Vietnamese to eventually relieve U.S. forces.[23]

Vice Admiral Elmo R. Zumwalt, Jr., upon assuming command as Commander Naval Forces, Vietnam, on 30 September 1968, concentrated on developing an accelerated plan to transfer U.S. Navy equipment to the South Vietnamese. In 1969, two South Vietnamese Navy lieutenants reported on board patrol boats, initiating the first phase of the turnover program. One month later, 17 South Vietnamese Navy ensigns and two lieutenants reported to Squadron One. On 16 May 1969, the USCGC *Point Garnet* (WPB-82310) and *Point League* (WPB-82304) were transferred to the South Vietnamese Navy at Saigon and renamed the *Le Phuoc Duc* and *Le Van Nga*, respectively. On 15 August 1970, the last of the 26 cutters were transferred to the South Vietnamese Navy. This ended the role of the 82-foot U.S. Coast Guard cutters in Vietnam.[24]

The statistics of Coast Guard Squadron One are impressive. The Coast Guard boarded 236,396 junks and sampans, inspected 283,527 vessels, participated in 4,461 naval gunfire missions, cruised 4,215,116 miles, damaged or destroyed 1,811 vessels, and wounded or killed 1,055 of the enemy. The Coast Guard casualties were seven killed and 53 wounded.[25] Most important, the cutters helped shift the enemy's supply route. General Westmoreland noted that before 1965 an estimated 70% of the enemy's supplies arrived by sea; "by the end of 1966, our best guess was not more than 10 percent" arrived by sea.[26]

The Coast Guard's involvement in Vietnam was not restricted to the 82-foot patrol boats. At sea, 56 different combat cutters, including high-endurance cutters, were assigned to Vietnamese waters. Noncombat cutters also participated in the war. For example, four buoy tenders and one cargo vessel were assigned to Vietnam. The buoy tenders assisted in aids-to-navigation duties, such as setting buoys and other markers for the safe navigation of ships. Shore units included port security, which supervised the loading and unloading of dangerous cargoes. Also, shipping advisers and Merchant Marine details helped merchant shipping.

But Operation Market Time proved the military ability of the U.S. Coast Guard. This small service was able to go from its peacetime role of search and rescue to war halfway around the world in less than 75 days. The Coast Guard performed and worked effectively with other services and played a major role in actions requiring small craft. In short, the U.S. Coast Guard proved the truth of *Semper Paratus*.

Notes

1. Information on the *Point Grey's* engagement from Commander, *Coast Guard Squadron One Diary*, 1–15 May 1966, Navy Operational Archives, Naval Historical Center, Washington, D.C.
2. James A. Hodgman, "Market Time in the Gulf of Thailand," *Proceedings*, May 1968, pp. 39–40; Commander, *Coast Guard Squadron One Diary*.
3. Information on the Point Ellis's engagement from Commander, *Coast Guard Squadron One Diary*, 14 March 1967.
4. R. L. Schreadley, "The Naval War in Vietnam, 1950–1970," *Proceedings*, May 1971, p. 182; W. C. Westmoreland, *Report on Operations in South Vietnam*, January 1964–June 1968 (Washington, D.C.: U.S. Government Printing Office, 1969), p. 128.
5. Westmoreland, pp. 87–88.
6. Schreadley, p. 187.
7. Schreadley, pp. 186–187; Eugene N. Tullich, *The United States Coast Guard in Southeast Asia During the Vietnam Conflict* (Washington, D.C.: Public Affairs Division, U.S. Coast Guard, 1975), p. 1.
8. Schreadley, p. 188.
9. Ibid.
10. The Brevie Line is the geographic division in the Gulf of Thailand between Vietnam and Cambodia. Islands and territorial waters to the north of that line are Cambodian and to the south, Vietnamese. Schreadley, p. 190.
11. Ibid.
12. Hodgman, pp. 39–40.
13. Hodgman, pp. 40–45; Tullich, pp. 3–5.
14. Schreadley, p. 190.

15. Tullich, p. 5.
16. Ibid.
17. Hodgman, p. 49.
18. Tullich, p. 6.
19. Hodgman, pp. 53–54.
20. Tullich, p. 12.
21. Ibid., pp. 6–8.
22. Information on the *Point Welcome* from Tullich, p. 10.
23. Schreadley, p. 191.
24. Schreadley, pp. 197–198; Tullich, pp. 14–15.
25. Tullich, p. 55.
26. Westmoreland, p. 128.

AUTHOR'S NOTE: *I wish to thank Professor Robert E. May, Department of History, and Kevin Reid, Department of History, Purdue University, for their helpful comments.*

Senior Chief Noble entered the U.S. Coast Guard in 1957 and retired in 1978 as a Senior Chief Marine Science Technician. He received bachelor's and master's degrees from the Catholic University of America, Washington, D.C. Since retirement, he has been the Director of the Delphi Public Library, Indiana, and he is studying for his doctorate degree in U.S. history at Purdue University. Senior Chief Noble is the coauthor of two books and author or coauthor of more than 20 articles.

10 "Ice in the Bering Sea and Arctic Ocean"

Commander F. A. Zeusler, USCG

U.S. Naval Institute *Proceedings*
(August 1941): 1102–6

THESE DATA ARE SUBMITTED as of interest to those navigators who cruise and patrol the Bering Sea and the Arctic Ocean. Conditions change constantly and seamen must govern themselves accordingly. In 1937 the ice conditions off Barrow and Nome were the worst in 20 years, while in 1940 they were the lightest. Hence, the various situations have to be met; but if the basic factors are known, it is easier to plan for any emergency that may arise than if the navigator gropes around in the dark.

The area between Nunivak Island in the Bering Sea and Point Barrow in the Arctic Ocean is covered with ice during certain periods of the year. Most of it is sea-water ice, but at certain periods it is also menaced with fresh-water ice from the rivers and the bays. From an oceanographic viewpoint, the ice effects in this area are as follows:

(a) By ice moving over the bottom the contours are changed.
(b) By ice moving along the coast some parts are eroded, while others are built up, thereby changing the coast line.
(c) Its presence affects the temperatures, salinities, and chemical contents of the waters carrying it.

(d) Its cooling and its freshening effect modifies the circulation of the water of the sea and so tends to modify or change the climate, especially along the coasts.

(e) The melting of the ice of the Yukon River and other rivers and bays causes to be deposited into the water much imbedded material, which in some cases is carried by the currents from place to place.

(f) Its presence acts as an impenetrable barrier to commerce in some sections, or is a temporary obstruction, necessitating changes in trade routes in others.

Some of the ice is transported into the areas where it is encountered, while some is actually formed there; hence in order to show the limitations and reasons for certain reactions the physical properties of sea water should be reviewed. Generally speaking, we are interested in the temperature, pressure, and saline content. The seagoing personnel realize its uselessness because of its bitter and salty taste, it being unsuited for drinking, cooking, and for washing; and yet these very defects of the water in varying degrees are responsible for the different amounts of ice formed.

Salt water can be considered to have the properties of a dilute solution of salt and when so compared with fresh water it is heavier, it has a lower freezing point, a higher boiling point, a higher electric conductivity, a higher viscosity, and a lower vapor tension.

The freezing point of sea water varies with the amount of the dissolved salts—the greater the saline content the lower the freezing point. The average freezing point is about 28.7° F. Sea water, unlike fresh water, is at its maximum density at the freezing point, but the ice expands at the moment of freezing and so floats.

The polar water areas, having a low salinity due to dilution by fresh water and to low evaporation, freeze very easily and in large sections. When the freezing point is reached in the bays and inlets and in the leads in the ice pack, ice begins to form. Strictly speaking, sea ice, although it freezes in the sea, is not in the last analysis frozen sea water because the freezing is a selective process in which about ⅘ of the saline matter is discarded, the solid product being almost fresh. The discarded salt liquid sinks by reason of its greater density and the ice floats. The first ice crystals are comparatively fresh because the pure water molecules tend to congeal first. Finally a solid mass of pure ice crystals is frozen together, interspersed with a small number of salt crystals, and a certain amount of brine which determines its salinity. Quick freezing means much trapping of salt crystals and so high salinity. Slower freezing and drainage results in loss of brine and so less of salinity. The water takes on an oily appearance due to the forming of ice needles which increase rapidly until it is covered with a layer of plastic ice. Those spike-like particles grow rapidly under cold quiet sea conditions and soon assume crystalline forms. With an undisturbed sea, the ice soon becomes strong enough to hold falling snow. This is called sludge. It continues to form a soupy consistency and takes on a leaden tint. The surface is never smooth and hard, but rough and sticky due to the precipitated salts. It soon loses its mobility in transmitting wave motion and it offers resistance to any vessel entering it. As there always is a slight undulating motion on the sea, the freezing finally concentrates into a number of centers and then spreads out from them. Bay ice is now forming. These centers are the middle of hexagonal sections 3" to 15" in diameter. Under the freezing process they become larger and larger until they reach about 3 feet in diameter. Gradually the sections are rolled up against one another by the motion of the sea and their edges are rounded and turned up, forming pancake ice. Continued cold causes the raised edges of the pancakes to thicken and to slowly cement one to another and the product is a sheet of young ice. There are in general three forms of sea ice caused by the continual breaking up and refreezing of the young ice: (a) glaucous, (b) floe ice, and (c) field ice.

Ice has been known to grow in thickness as much as five inches in eight hours, its rate of growth depending on the air temperature, the salinity, and the wind velocity. Tests show its tensile strength to be less than that of fresh-water ice on account of the salt crystals. A heavy snow covering often delays the growth by preventing the passage of heat through the ice. The freezing of ice does not necessarily stop during the summer. The sun's warmth melts the surface snow which runs off into the sea. Often this reduces the surface temperature low enough for new ice to form under the layers of the old ice. There have been cases where at the end of the summer the ice was thicker than at the beginning, even with the surface ice melting. In autumn this process ceases and the growth does not begin again until the lower temperatures of winter cool the surface layers of the sea. The actual level of the ice is often below the water line, due to the weight of the accumulated snow. When this happens the surface layers are flooded. The sea water mixing there with the snow produces a solution of lower salinity and higher freezing point and in this case the floe will add to its thickness by growth from above, but the usual method of growth is by the formation of ice crystals to the under surface of the floe.

The formation of fast (or shore) ice hinders the freezing of the sea to any great depth, as the ice is a bad conductor of heat and so prevents the loss of heat from the underlying water by radiation and also because the salts given up from the fast ice make the underlying water of higher salinity and hence a lower freezing point. Snow also, being a bad conductor of heat, its coefficient being $\frac{1}{10}$ of that of ice, assists in preventing the freezing to any great depth.

Sea ice is in constant danger of breaking up at all times and drifts under the influence of tide, wind, current, and sea. Hence drifting sea ice may be driven on the beach or up against stationary ice, or against very slowly drifting floes. When floes, cakes, etc., are forced over the others or turned end on end, it is called rafting. The greater the disturbance, the greater the rafting. Heavier and thicker ice will be formed.

Often field ice will drift from shore or will separate, forming leads or passages through the ice area. Detached hummocks are called floebergs. These should not be confused with icebergs, or growlers, which are of glacial origin. Pressure ridges are formed by a very large external loose floe riding upon a fixed floe or upon the shore under the pressure of the wind or the current. They are higher near the shore and lower at the sea end.

The ice encountered in the Pacific Arctic comes under the following classifications: (a) the Arctic pack, (b) pack ice, (c) shore or fast ice. The Arctic pack is the core of that vast ice area that occupies the Arctic regions. It is that permanent ice sector which moves north and south generally and east and west occasionally under the influence of wind and current. It is a solid hummocky ice, maintained from year to year by the falling snow, by the rafting of pack ice, and by freezing. It consists generally of large fields of old rafted pack ice and possesses great thickness, solidity, area, and power. Its edges usually disintegrate during the summer months, but it seems to hold its general size and strength, by the building up on it by the pack ice whenever the conditions are favorable for it. It suffers as much from the summer heat, the summer gales, and the attendant seas as the other types of ice.

Inshore of the Arctic pack is the pack ice. This is rafted and frozen shore ice, and is generally covered with snow. It is in large fields but does not have the thickness, solidity, area, and power of the Arctic pack. It usually contains many pans and some medium-sized fields with few leads. It is hummocky and contains many pools of water, and if the ice is not rotten the water is practically fresh and is a source of good drinking water. The Coast Guard cutter *Northland* took water from four of the pools observed. In one hole, 10 feet wide, about 15 feet long, and 7 feet deep, the first foot of water contained less than two grains of salt, the second foot contained from 2–4 grains, the third 4–7 grains, the fourth 7–9, the fifth 12 grains, while the bottom contained 40–50 grains. Pack ice is destroyed when it drifts into the lower latitudes with their relatively warm waters. Surface melting due to summer sun is not unusual. Floes on the outer edge of the pack are broken into small pieces by ocean swells. These pieces have their temperatures raised and thus disintegration is rapid for the ice becomes soft and pliable and quickly melts. Partial melting in a floe produces a honey-combed effect. The wreckage of the pack on the edge of the sea is called brash and is ordinarily not dangerous to a vessel unless it comes into contact with the propeller.

Inshore of the pack ice is the freshly-frozen ice, which is known as the fast (or shore) ice. It freezes anew each year from about December first and increases in thickness until the end of April. This is usually found from Barrow south to Nunivak Island, from the shore to the pack ice. The alignment of ice to seaward is shore-foot, fast ice, pack ice, Arctic pack. With the advent of summer, the shore ice breaks adrift under the action of wind, tide, current, and sea, and through the increases in air temperatures during the months of June, July, and August. During the month of June the northern trek of the Arctic pack begins. The Bering Strait opens up under a strong northerly current. Leads are formed in the pack ice and in the shore ice, with a result that the elements cause disintegration and consequent breaking away of the shore ice from the land. As soon as there is a clearing in the Bering Strait, the disintegrated shore ice and pack ice from the southward moves to the northward. A great deal of shore ice is melted and some of it is disintegrated through the action of the sea, while some of it is grafted onto pack ice. Similarly some of the pack ice is destroyed, disintegrated, and melted, and so the status quo is maintained by nature.

About the time the break occurs in the Bering Strait the ice of Norton Sound, Norton Bay, and Yukon Flats menaces the waters south of Bering Straits following the fast ice and pack ice in their trek to the northward.

The pack ice reaches as far south as St. Lawrence Island. With its recession to the northward much of the Siberian shore ice southwest of St. Lawrence Island menaces the waters off the northwestern shore of that island. The Arctic pack ice seldom reaches much below the Arctic Circle, but many loose pieces of Arctic pack ice can be seen throughout the area that is occupied by the pack ice. By July 15 the pack ice has moved northward materially and the area around King Island is covered completely by Yukon, Norton Bay, and Norton Sound ice. Some of this ice is found off Icy Cape during the first part of August, but as a whole mostly pack ice and Arctic pack ice are encountered in those waters. The prevailing northwest winds keep the pack on the Alaskan side and so there is seldom much pack ice on the Siberian side.

In the Bering Sea the western side of the pack is open before the Romanzof side but it is questionable whether one can get into Nome sooner via the western leads without danger. The trip to Bering Strait can be negotiated sooner from the Siberian shore. Both shores are clear of ice. This is probably due in part to the land breezes which blow from each shore during the spring months and to the discharge of fresh water from the streams from both shores. This water is heated by the sun and by the warm banks so that it is not unusual to see 35°, even 36°, with ice all around. The ice in the rivers generally breaks up before that of the sea and, being drifted out by the current, forces its way through the sea ice for miles. It is, therefore, a safe procedure that in approaching Nome from the southward and upon investigating the southern limits of the ice, if blue ice is found in the normal course to Nome, attempting leads to the westward would be futile as that would steer the vessel into the pack. Hence cruising to the eastward alone is safest and there is no danger of being caught in the pack and drifting with it to the northward. If dirty ice is seen, which indicates ice from the rivers and shores, then leads east or west are safe as long as the vessel remains in the discolored ice. The floe remains longest in the eddy north of St. Lawrence Island. It moves in a rotary motion until blown out by winds into the north-going current.

Movement of ice.—Ice is moved by the wind with the aid of the currents. A clearing at Point Barrow, at Wainwright, and at the Sea Horses is dependent directly on the flow of the current to the northward. When this current ceases to flow, there is nothing that can possibly open up the heavy ice that is usually found at the Sea Horses. The light ice at Barrow and Wainwright will drift with the wind. Northerly winds close up Barrow and the section as far south as Icy Cape. Northeast winds have a tendency to open up the whole area and these winds in conjunction with a strong northerly current soon clear out the ice, driving the Arctic pack offshore and the loose pack ice northward. Easterly winds and southeasterly winds have a tendency to open up the channel off the Sea Horses. South winds drive the ice in on Point Franklin. However, winds from the southern quadrant are desirable for a period of time to begin the flow of the northerly currents. West and northwest winds drive the ice onshore throughout the whole sector.

It is the Arctic pack that closes the polar seas to navigation and guards the inner secrets of the Arctic basin. A vessel can safely penetrate drift or loose pack ice, but the ordinary wooden or steel vessel without super-strengthening or proper wooden sheathing runs a risk if caught in the Arctic floes. A steel ice breaker and a well-constructed wooden vessel built for polar work are on a par, especially if the vessel is small, has fairly high power and protected propellers. The danger lies not in meeting loose floes, but in being caught in the pack ice drifting before a strong wind or in a closing lead. This may result in the vessel being imprisoned in the pack. Safety depends on her ability to rise under pressure, the ice meeting below and lifting the vessel out of the water. If this does not happen and the pressure does not slacken, the vessel will be crushed.

When the ice is reached it usually becomes necessary to cruise along the edge to find a lead. Whoever is piloting goes to the crow's-nest and seeks out a favorable opening. Extreme caution must be used in entering the lead. The weather, currents, appearance of ice, probable winds, the condition of the ship, and its handling ability must be taken into consideration before the ice is entered. The ship must be kept clear of dangers ahead, and the movements of the ice in all directions must be watched. If the lead has a tendency to close up, the vessel must get out as soon as possible for fear of being crushed or it may be caught in the ice, drifting to the northward, with a possibility of having to abandon her. It should be remembered that a swell encountered in the ice is always an indicator of open water. The ice blink is usually indicative of ice while the rather bluish margin of ice indicates open water.

Ice is struck bow on and shattered. The more solid ice should not be struck, because it might damage the vessel, but it should be approached slowly and the pieces pushed out of the way. A good ice man will not nose his ship through ice that is impenetrable although he will go through narrow lanes, first getting the starboard bow against a piece and shoving it clear, then pushing another piece aside with the port bow, etc.

The ship is often brought to a standstill by the heavy ice with the engines going ahead full speed, but by persistence bit by bit the heavy floes begin to rotate and so finally by their motion and momentum clear a way through which the ship can steam ahead. Engines are stopped often to prevent the broken ice from getting into the wheel. Often heavy floes meet at two points and there is open water beyond. Swinging the ship is impossible. The engines are stopped and then reversed. After going a certain distance astern, full speed ahead is given. The ship charges full speed toward the narrowest part and, when the impact is made, it trembles from bow to stern, the mast shakes violently, the personnel are almost thrown off their feet, and what appears most disconcerting, there is no visible effect on the ice. This operation is repeated until the neck is finally broken and the ship then passes into clear water.

11   "More Assets for the Arctic"

Captain Lawson Brigham, USCG (Ret.)

U.S. Naval Institute *Proceedings*
(December 2015): 30–35

BY ANY MEASURE 2015 was a challenging and highly successful year for U.S. Coast Guard polar operations and the nation's two polar ice-breakers, the USCGC *Polar Star* (WAGB-10) and *Healy* (WAGB-20). Dialogue is continuing on how to rebuild the nation's polar icebreaker fleet, with President Barack Obama weighing in on the issue in September during his visit to Alaska and in a White House Fact Sheet announcing new federal Arctic investments, including icebreakers.[1] Likely not since the time of President Franklin D. Roosevelt's request during World War II for a U.S. icebreaker fleet has a U.S. President been personally and directly involved in such issues.[2]

Deployments to the polar ends of the world showcase today's global maritime reach of the United States provided by Coast Guard polar icebreakers. Recapping the operational year, the *Polar Star* and *Healy* supported multiple U.S. agencies in their polar work and a major international ocean-research program. A notable search-and-rescue operation was executed in a remote region with difficult Antarctic sea ice conditions. The *Healy* completed the first U.S. unaccompanied icebreaker transit to the North Pole as well as the cutter's third visit there, but the

122

first since 2005. These highly successful operations in Antarctic waters and across the central Arctic Ocean basin visibly demonstrate how an effective icebreaker capacity can provide reliable and unambiguous U.S. polar maritime presence.

Unique National Maritime Assets

Coast Guard polar icebreakers are instruments of national policy and the visible, sovereign presence of the United States in Arctic and Antarctic waters. They are foremost capital maritime and naval assets of the U.S. government that historically have supported a host of federal agencies. Operating independently in the polar regions where the United States has broad national interests, these specialized naval vessels can provide the commander-in-chief and the unified combatant commanders—the Northern and Pacific Commands would be the obvious potential Department of Defense users—a unique polar capability that is undeniably an integral component of American naval and maritime power. No other surface ships in the U.S. National Fleet (a joint U.S. Navy and Coast Guard concept and effort to address commonality and interoperability) can operate safely and effectively anywhere on the global oceans *and* along the relatively uncharted coastal waters of the Arctic and Antarctic. Surface and subsurface combatants rarely operate in these high-risk and shallow coastal waters, making a Coast Guard icebreaker the sole U.S. maritime and naval presence in those areas.

A U.S. polar icebreaker must also be viewed as a Coast Guard cutter with an inherent design that allows effective operation in all types of sea ice along with sustained on-scene presence and assured polar marine access. Cutters such as the *Polar Star* and *Healy* are essentially mobile Coast Guard multi-mission bases or platforms with long-range endurance in all polar marine regions. Ship-based mobility and the agility and flexibility to respond in the face of rapidly changing sea ice and other polar environmental conditions are an icebreaker's greatest assets.

A commanding officer of these ships holds a wide range of legal authorities and responsibilities identical to all Coast Guard cutter commanders. That same captain also leads an independent marine operation with all its logistical challenges to the far reaches of the planet, providing the United States with a key global maritime capability. Every officer who has served on board one of these cutters understands the singular importance of this strategic requirement. A review of the types of missions with which a captain might be tasked on a polar deployment is instructive. Several examples illustrate a complex suite of plausible missions:

- Conducting Coast Guard statutory missions (such as law enforcement; search and rescue; marine safety; marine environmental protection; aids to navigation; defense readiness; ports, waterways, and coastal security; and more) in U.S. and international waters. Of importance, all cutters are the primary U.S. maritime law-enforcement presence at sea.

- Enforcing U.S. law and sovereign rights in the U.S. territorial sea, contiguous zone, and exclusive economic zone. Operations could include enforcing U.S. law on American vessels and citizens who might be operating in Antarctic waters for research, contract work, or adventure tourism.

- Responding to high-latitude incidents, emergencies, and potential maritime disasters from ships or marine operations associated with offshore development such as exploratory drilling. In such circumstances an icebreaker acts as the U.S. government's on-scene presence for command and control and can provide icebreaking in support of unlocking frozen harbors and waterways to facilitate commercial supply access.

- Conducting science and research in the national interest in the most demanding and remote regions at both ends of the world. Expeditions could include polar marine-transportation research and development in support of future systems for the U.S. maritime Arctic.

- Conducting bathymetric and scientific surveys north of Alaska to support a future U.S. extended continental shelf claim under the provisions of Article 76 of the United Nations Convention on the Law of the Sea and more traditional bathymetric surveying along select routes within the U.S. maritime Arctic.

- Working in concert with U.S. and foreign polar research vessels and assuring access to remote survey locations that only a few of the world's icebreakers can reach.

- Serving as an integral element of a support and search-and-rescue network for U.S. naval operations *and* DOD research in the Arctic Ocean. Support to the DOD can include icebreaking operations along the western coast of Greenland to the U.S. northernmost defense facilities at Thule Air Base.

- Acting as a mobile observation platform in all polar marine environments and during long transits of the global ocean and providing ocean and atmospheric data to ground truth satellite and aerial observations. Support to such agencies as NOAA, the National Science Foundation (NSF), the National Air and Space Administration, and the DOD for polar environmental observation has been long-standing.

- Conducting icebreaking operations in support of the U.S. Antarctic Program, led by the NSF, such as the seasonal breakout of the McMurdo base for resupply-ship access and conducting Antarctic Treaty inspections around the continent led by the Department of State.

Notably, all of these missions have been conducted by Coast Guard polar icebreakers in recent decades during an era of fewer ships and an aging fleet. The current imperative to replace these capital assets is what the President addressed during his visit to Alaska. Announced were his plans to accelerate acquisition of additional icebreakers, with mention of a key caveat for multiple ships that can operate year-round in the Arctic

Ocean.[3] This is a significant high-end operational requirement that suggests new icebreakers would be among the largest and most powerful afloat. Viewed from strategic and global perspectives, such ships could also conduct all current and future U.S. icebreaking requirements in the Antarctic.

Links to Arctic Marine Transportation

There is considerable misunderstanding about the future use of the Arctic Ocean for marine transportation and the potential role of icebreakers as facilitators of marine traffic. Using a scenarios or futures effort, the Arctic Council's Arctic Marine Shipping Assessment (AMSA) released in 2009 found that the primary driver for Arctic navigation is the development of onshore and offshore natural resources and many links to global commodities markets (and prices).[4] Another finding was that the profound Arctic sea ice retreat being observed in all seasons is important to navigation in that it provides greater marine access and potentially longer seasons of navigation.

However, also key is that the Arctic Ocean remains fully or partially ice-covered for nearly eight to nine months each year. It is not an ice-free ocean, and one plausible navigation season will likely be three to four months in summer along the entire length of the Northern Sea Route (NSR) from Kara Gate to the Bering Strait; year-round navigation has been maintained for more than three decades in the western areas of the Russian Arctic.[5]

In an effort to build a reliable and safe national Arctic waterway, Russia employs a fleet of large nuclear- and diesel-powered icebreakers for use in convoying and ice escort of commercial ships that are primarily carrying natural resources out of the Russian Arctic to global markets. However, even Russian maritime experts state that the NSR is a seasonal complement to a route using the Suez Canal around Eurasia.[6] Few believe the NSR will become a trans-Arctic container-shipping route, primarily limited by its seasonality of access and overall environmental challenges that have an impact on reliability.[7]

Two highly relevant issues are influencing the possible operation of government-owned icebreakers for potential ice convoy in the Arctic marine areas of the United States and Canada. One issue is technical: the emergence of highly capable icebreaking commercial carriers that operate independently without the need for icebreaker escort. This is the likely future operational mode that is economically viable for commercial ships throughout the Arctic Ocean. These advanced icebreaking cargo ships have successfully sailed in the Russian maritime Arctic, including the NSR, and within the Canadian Arctic and through the Northwest Passage. The second issue relates to national policy and the future establishment of U.S. and Canadian Arctic marine transportation systems that could require escort or convoy icebreakers to extend the ice-navigation season beyond summer.

Would the two governments provide Coast Guard icebreakers for routine escort duties if many of the ships being supported do not trade in U.S. and Canadian supports? Such a scenario would seem problematic and a viable alternative would be to have privately owned icebreakers chartered to support commercial shippers where and when required. While the justification of new U.S. Coast Guard icebreakers is clearly not based on convoying commercial ships in open Arctic seas, these ships would be available for response operations and potentially for the breakout of ports and coastal waterways (such as is conducted on the Great Lakes and in the U.S. northeast).

Past Polar Icebreaker Studies

In July 1984 the Coast Guard released a major interagency assessment, the *United States Polar Icebreaker Requirements Study* (*PIRS*), which had been mandated by the Office of Management and Budget.[8] This key analysis has remained a framework document on U.S. polar icebreaker issues for three decades. It provided the historical context for U.S. polar ships that have operated in Alaska since its purchase from Russia in 1867, in war-time theaters such as Greenland during World War II, and in the

Antarctic since the early 20th century. The report affirmed the need to replace aging *Wind*-class icebreakers with new polar icebreakers operated by the Coast Guard.

A fleet of four icebreakers was recommended to meet a broad range of strategic and bipolar national interests. *PIRS* was updated in 1990 by a Presidential Report to Congress, which concluded that a fleet of the two *Polar*-class ships and an NSF polar research vessel should be joined by a new polar icebreaker with enhanced research capabilities. This report was the impetus for Congress to fund construction of the *Healy*, which was commissioned in 2000.

A high-level committee of the National Research Council released an authoritative and comprehensive study of future U.S. polar icebreaker needs in 2007.[9] It contains strong recommendations that the United States must continue an active and influential presence in the Arctic and Antarctic and maintain a fleet of Coast Guard polar icebreakers. Again, this study called for the renewal of the nation's polar icebreaker fleet.

In 2010 a report prepared for the Coast Guard by outside consultants—the *United States Coast Guard High Latitude Region Mission Analysis*, using operations-research modeling—concluded that to meet its statutory polar missions the service would require three heavy and three medium icebreakers. More ships would be needed (a mix of six heavy and four medium icebreakers) if a requirement for continuous polar presence was maintained consistent with a joint Naval Operations Concept developed that year. The bottom line for all of these studies is the need for the U.S. government to operate a fleet of Coast Guard polar icebreakers to meet our broad national interests in the emerging Arctic and Antarctic. All of these studies are consistent in recommending three or more highly capable Coast Guard polar icebreakers for global operations.

Federal Budget Challenges

In an era of multiple congressional budget constraints, the funding for even a single new polar icebreaker (at $800–900 million) is complex. It has been very difficult for the administration and Congress to identify a viable and fundable long-term strategy for icebreaker procurement. A significant challenge the Coast Guard has confronted for decades, even when under the Department of Transportation, has been the size of its acquisition, construction, and improvements account. That cannot easily accommodate partial funding identified for a polar icebreaker, given the range of cutter, aircraft, and shoreside assets that require renewal and replacement.

The Coast Guard, with a strongly held view that a polar icebreaker is a national asset with multiple agency users, seeks to have significant funding contributions from other agencies. This could only come about by those agencies' deferral or cancellation of a host of future acquisitions such as aircraft, ships, weapons, satellites, research equipment, and more. It is important to remember that procurement of the *Healy* was accomplished with non–Coast Guard funding solely from the Navy's shipbuilding account. A more equitable strategy must be found. Others are pursuing alternative strategies to somehow reduce or defer funding for polar icebreakers:

- Funding the reactivation of the USCGC *Polar Sea* (WAGB-11) as a stopgap measure while new ships are under construction.
- Investigating strategies to build an icebreaker in a foreign shipyard (today likely illegal without Presidential intervention, and doubtless politically unacceptable).
- Pursuit of leasing arrangements of polar icebreakers with the private sector (notably the entire cost of a long-term federal lease must be identified up front; such leases are likely more expensive to the federal government and the taxpayer).

One plausible future strategy may be incremental increases in the Homeland Security/Coast Guard budget for icebreaker acquisition with costs spread over a broad suite of stakeholder agencies. This would surely require a directive from President Obama or his successor. Action even today would create a several-year gap in the operation of the nation's most capable icebreaker while awaiting the commissioning of a new ship.

Looking Forward

Multiple interagency, independent, and Coast Guard assessments—and more than three decades of debate—have highlighted the strategic needs for U.S. government–owned polar icebreakers best operated by the Coast Guard. With a rapidly changing Arctic and rising marine use in the region, these requirements have increased, providing greater strategic clarity on this issue. The U.S. Arctic policy statement in 2009 and a *National Strategy for the Arctic Region* issued in 2013 have reinforced our national interests in the area. Most would agree that our national polar (maritime) interests are not well served by outsourcing them to foreign governments. Nor are these same strategic needs met by potentially available (but less capable) domestic or foreign-flag commercial icebreaking ships that lack the robust, multi-mission capacity of Coast Guard icebreakers.

The time for further study and continued debate about U.S. polar icebreakers is over, as surmised by President Obama and his Executive Office team, with action taken as far back as a Fiscal Year 2013 budget submission to initiate an icebreaker-procurement process. A "whole of government" approach responding to this deficit and funding these national assets is still required to harness interagency and congressional support and limit parochial interests and budgetary rivalry. A recent clarion call in Washington and the current U.S. chairmanship of the Arctic Council reminds Americans that we are an Arctic nation.

A strong signal is also needed to remind all of us that America, as a leading and influential polar nation, continues to have critical strategic interests and key investment needs in both polar regions throughout the 21st century. Few requirements are more important than modern Coast Guard icebreakers that maintain our global maritime capability, assure polar marine access, and provide visible, effective U.S. maritime presence.

Notes

1. "Fact Sheet: President Obama Announces New Investments to Enhance Safety and Security in the Changing Arctic," (The White House, 1 September 2015), www.whitehouse.gov/the-press-office/2015/09/02/fact-sheet-president-obama-announcesnew-investments-combat-climate.

2. *Polar Icebreakers in a Changing World: An Assessment of U.S. Needs,* (Washington, DC: National Research Council of the National Academies, 2007), 54. www.nap.edu/read/11753/chapter/1.

3. "Fact Sheet: President Obama Announces New Investments," 1 September 2015.

4. Arctic Marine Shipping Assessment, (Arctic Council, April 2009), www.pame.is.

5. CAPT Lawson W. Brigham, USCG, (Ret.), "Russia Opens Its Maritime Arctic," U.S. Naval Institute *Proceedings*, vol. 137, no. 5 (May 2011), 50–55.

6. "Northern Sea Route Slated for Massive Growth," *The Moscow Times,* 4 June 2013, www.themoscowtimes.com/business/article/northern-sea-route-slated-for-massive-growth/481093.html.

7. Steven M. Carmel, "The Cold, Hard Realities of Arctic Shipping," U.S. Naval Institute *Proceedings*, vol. 139, no. 7 (July 2013), 38–41.

8. "United States Polar Icebreaker Requirements Study, Interagency Report," U.S. Coast Guard. Washington, DC, 11 July 1984, www.nap.edu/read/11753/chapter/18#114.

9. *Polar Icebreakers in a Changing World: An Assessment of U.S. Needs,* 54.

Captain Brigham is distinguished professor of geography and arctic policy at the University of Alaska Fairbanks and a Fellow at the U.S. Coast Guard Academy's Center for Arctic Study and Policy. He earned a PhD from the University of Cambridge in 2000 and commanded four cutters, including the USCGC *Polar Sea* on Arctic and Antarctic voyages. He served as chair of the Arctic Council's Arctic Marine Shipping Assessment from 2005–2009.

12 "Exporting Coast Guard Expertise"

James Loy and Bruce Stubbs

U.S. Naval Institute *Proceedings*
(May 1997): 55–57

WHEN COAST GUARD INVOLVEMENT in international programs is discussed, thoughts normally drift down to the Caribbean and Latin America. Our contributions to counternarcotics and illegal migrant activities in that region are well storied, but there are other areas of the world where Coast Guard involvement could add real value to the attainment of U.S. objectives. Long the recipient of Mobile Training Team visits, and more recently the scene of much instability following the breakup of the Soviet Union, the European theater is such an area.

In the summer of 1995, the Coast Guard cutter *Dallas* (WHEC-716) conducted an unprecedented deployment to the Mediterranean and Black seas. The following year, the *Gallatin* (WHEC-721) deployed to the Baltic to become the first cutter to participate in the annual BaltOps exercise. These deployments supported the goal of the Commander-in-Chief, U.S. European Command (CinCEur), to promote regional stability by engaging key littoral nations in a wider variety of naval and maritime activities more suitable to the requirements of the post–Cold War world. They also highlighted the Coast Guard's emerging role in providing relevant, complementary capabilities to help attain the objectives of the U.S. National Security Strategy of engagement and enlargement.

Based on the Coast Guard's multimission character and successful involvement in the international community, CinCEur and U.S. Naval Forces, European Command (USNavEur), have developed requirements for Coast Guard forces. Both want the service to support the maritime component of their theater engagement strategy by participating in such activities as military-to-military contacts, professional exchanges, international organizations and agreements, technical and security assistance, operational deployments, combined operations and exercises, and port visits. In addition, the U.S. European Command (USEuCom) has a continuing requirement for Coast Guard support of contingency plans for coastal sea control, harbor defense, and port security.

CinCEur's overarching theater strategic goals are to promote stability and prevent aggression. One principal concept to promote stability is to "engage in peacetime," using military resources in nontraditional ways to mold the security environment toward peacekeeping objectives and enhance security cooperation and interaction. Three programs of significant application to the Coast Guard are the International Military and Education Training Program (IMET), Partnership for Peace, and the Joint Contact Team Program.

One part of the International Military and Education Training Program involves Coast Guard Mobile Training Teams (MTTs), which enable the Coast Guard to train other nations' maritime services in a variety of technical issues using the equipment and facilities of the host nation. The International Training Division at Yorktown, Virginia—the center of MTT efforts—can deploy teams around the world in all Coast Guard mission areas. During fiscal year 1996, MTTs conducted training in 45 countries at the request of the Departments of Defense and State.

The other half of IMET is the resident training program, which allows foreign students to study at Coast Guard specialty schools in the United States. Since 1942, international students from more than 110 countries have attended Coast Guard resident schools. There currently are 72 courses available that expose the students to many aspects of Coast

Guard operations; more than one-third of the students take advantage of their time here to get on-the-job training with our operational units.

While enrolled in Coast Guard schools, international students have an opportunity to learn about American culture and institutions and our commitment to human rights. The International Maritime Officers Course was developed recently in response to congressional requests to expand military training opportunities under IMET, to include democracy, military justice, and human rights. In fiscal year 1996, the Coast Guard was able to train personnel from 79 countries through resident training courses.

Begun in 1992, Partnership for Peace primarily is a multilateral NATO exercise program directed at central European and former Soviet republics. Its primary objectives are to facilitate national defense planning and budgeting, develop democratic control of defense forces, maintain the ability and willingness to contribute to common security requirements, foster cooperative military relations with NATO, and develop forces that are better able to operate with NATO members in humanitarian missions, search and rescue, and peacekeeping operations. Partnership for Peace liaison teams use familiarization tours, ship visits, conferences, and personnel exchanges to accomplish their mission. As of October 1996, the Coast Guard had conducted 44 such events in its mission areas, each one fully funded by USEuCom.

Why Is the Coast Guard Engaged Outside Our Shores?

The Coast Guard's reputation as a multimission law enforcement, humanitarian, and regulatory agency—with an unthreatening military presence—makes it well suited for the maritime diplomacy role of engagement. Most of the world's navies conduct functions in the coastal or contiguous seas. They are not blue-water, power-projection, sea-control navies—but rather regional navies that also enforce laws, protect resources, conduct search and rescue, prevent environmental damage, and maintain aids to navigation. These navies resemble the Coast Guard in everything but name, and they readily relate to the Coast Guard because of similarities in force mix and missions.

In the March 1995 International Navies issue of *Proceedings*, 29 commanders of the world's navies commented on what makes their forces relevant today. Eighteen mentioned Coast Guard–equivalent missions such as search and rescue, environmental protection, fisheries protection, and law enforcement as part of their taskings.

The Coast Guard is the right instrument to supplement current U.S. efforts to engage maritime nations, especially those the United States would like to influence. During the November 1995 meeting of the Navy–Coast Guard Board, the Vice Chief of Naval Operations commented on the successful deployment of the *Dallas* to the Mediterranean and Black seas: "Cutter *Dallas* was a tremendous success. The Commission on Roles and Missions directed services to look at better options for engagement; this is right in line with that. Many navies want to look like the U.S. Navy . . . but showing them a cutter like *Dallas* might be just right for them."

Both USEuCom and USNavEur believe in the complementary value and relevancy of the Coast Guard in supporting their objective of promoting regional stability. Collectively, these two commands affirmed that the Coast Guard can:

- Act as a role model for emerging democratic nations in providing maritime services—most do not want high-end, high-tech warfighting navies
- Build stable and useful maritime services for these nations, showing them how to develop multimission maritime agencies rather than potentially destabilizing warfighting navies
- Engage host nations' existing navies or maritime services without overwhelming them
- Access multiple ministries of a host nation beyond the defense ministry, opening up many more doors to enduring relationships

A senior USEuCom staff officer summed it up this way: "You're the right force to reach the majority of the navies, especially the [Partnership for Peace] navies; what these countries need and can afford is a Coast Guard–like array of missions and associated force structure. The Coast Guard is an excellent example of civilian control of the military and how to merge together an agency with military and civilian duties."

There are, however, some impediments to using the Coast Guard. There are more demands for its services than can be met. Not everyone in the administration or Congress understands why the Coast Guard should operate overseas at all. Given the CinCs' requirements for Coast Guard services, there must be wider congressional and administration support of the Coast Guard's engagement role. Decision makers outside the service are not sure if or to what extent the Coast Guard should play. They see engagement as competing against what they consider to be the Coast Guard's true or traditional missions, and they don't recognize the Coast Guard's value as an instrument of national security, both at home and abroad.

The Coast Guard must lead the way in articulating the value of its role in and contribution to the national security goal of engagement. It must include such topics as scope, level of effort, and the relationship of the Coast Guard's own International Activities Program to the engagement strategies of the unified commanders, and it must consider what level of effort will be acceptable to the service's political and congressional leadership. This articulation must be communicated both internally and externally, to provide terms of reference for these efforts and to drive the development of a long-term Coast Guard International Strategic Plan. Such efforts currently are under way under the direction of the international affairs staff, with the participation of the area commanders.

The Coast Guard's contributions need to be mentioned and discussed in key national security documents. They need to be endorsed in unified commanders' congressional testimony. Coast Guard Headquarters staff and appropriate area staffs should be on formal distribution lists for the CinCs' regional campaign plans and individual country plans, for review and input of Coast Guard capabilities where applicable. An annual report of Coast Guard support activities by each unified commander would help to document Coast Guard contributions. Such initiatives are under way.

The Coast Guard Atlantic and Pacific Areas have a major responsibility to conduct international activities and to provide support to the unified commanders. Coast Guard Atlantic Area uses a theater engagement campaign—based on the policy direction contained in the Commandant's Strategic International Plan and guidance from the Commandant's International Advisory Group—to execute its strategy. The resulting plan for action calls for the employment of Atlantic Area forces to:

- Expand U.S. interaction with littoral nations beyond traditional DoD contact
- Expand U.S. presence and contact with those nations for which U.S. Navy presence is not yet appropriate

Using port visits, professional exchanges, operational deployments, combined operations, and military-to-military events, this campaign plan leverages unique Coast Guard capabilities to complement and expand U.S. maritime peacetime engagement efforts. It also stresses the Coast Guard as a role model for developing nations.

With the end of the Cold War, the Coast Guard's national defense mission has taken on a new slant. No longer a naval reserve augmentation force for convoy protection and coastal U.S. security, the Coast Guard now is contributing to national defense with relevant, complementary, and unique capabilities. The heart of this contribution is the expeditionary force designed for port security and harbor defense under the U.S. maritime defense zones. Peacetime engagement is a valuable addition to this role.

The 1995 and 1996 deployments of the *Dallas* and *Gallatin* have generated many new ideas and new ways to incorporate Coast Guard capabilities to help the unified commanders accomplish their strategic goals. The Coast Guard has the opportunity—perhaps the responsibility— to export its expertise abroad; the challenge now will be one of prioritization and continued legitimacy. Senior DoD commanders and their staffs are becoming more knowledgeable about the Coast Guard and strongly support its role as an instrument of national security. We have much to offer. It is up to us to communicate that wisely.

Admiral Loy is Chief of Staff, U.S. Coast Guard, and Commanding Officer, U.S. Coast Guard Headquarters. He previously served as Commander, Atlantic Area, and Commander, U.S. Maritime Defense Zone Atlantic, and has commanded four Coast Guard cutters, including 43 combat patrols in Vietnam. **Captain Stubbs,** a graduate of the Naval War College, recently served as the Chief of the Major Cutter Force Branch on the staff of the Atlantic Area Commander. He has served on the staff of the National Security Council and as a commanding officer of the *Harriet Lane* (WMEC-903).

13 "The Coast Guard *Is* Maritime Security"

James M. Loy

U.S. Naval Institute *Proceedings*
(December 1998): 26–29

FOR MORE THAN 200 YEARS the Coast Guard has provided the United States with a unique blend of humanitarian, law enforcement, and military capabilities. From the earliest duties of the Revenue Cutter Service in 1790, our core roles have expanded to include protecting the public, the environment, and U.S. economic and security interests in any maritime region in which U.S. interests may be in jeopardy.

The complexity of the tasks and the seriousness of the threats that confront us on the cusp of our next century of service are daunting: tight budgets, aging platforms, and constrained personnel force structure, along with increasing requirements. Although we are mindful of our core philosophy—*Semper Paratus*, Always Ready—perhaps at no other time in our history have we been asked to do more with less. More than simply "guarding the coast," the Coast Guard has broad responsibilities for safeguarding the global commons and brings unique humanitarian, law enforcement, and military capabilities to respond to the nation's hemispheric maritime security needs.

U.S. Maritime Security Interests . . .

Waterborne trade is the lifeblood of the U.S. economy. Ships carry raw materials and finished goods to and from every corner of the world, with key ports along the Atlantic, Gulf, and Pacific coasts serving as our gateways to the world. One quarter of all domestic goods is shipped by water, and half of all oil consumed in the United States arrives by sea. In 1997, some 90% of U.S. foreign trade by tonnage—valued at nearly $1.7 trillion—moved by ship. U.S. oceanborne exports have increased 50% since 1990, a trend that is expected to continue. Ironic for a country so tied to the sea and dependent on sea power to protect national interests, the U.S. merchant marine is ranked only 15th in the world, and it carries no more than 3% of U.S. oceanborne foreign trade.

This has potentially grave implications for U.S. military readiness, in addition to global economic competitiveness. Almost all of the equipment, ordnance, and supplies needed to support any sizable projection of military power must move by sea. During the Gulf War, nearly 95% of all material sent to the combat theater—and returned to the United States once peace was restored—was carried on ships. Efficient ports are critical to U.S. military combat operations, as well as to crisis response and humanitarian missions. They also are crucial if the U.S. strategy of engagement is to succeed.

Increased use of the oceans for recreation, fishing, minerals development, and transportation guarantees greater stresses on the marine environment and can pose grave risks to U.S. interests. Globally, critical fish stocks are under great pressure, as overfishing and habitat destruction continue. Living marine resources support a $20 billion commercial industry. Tourism and marine recreation—alone worth millions of dollars to state and local economies each year—likewise demand clean shorelines and marine environments. At the same time, new technologies are permitting more remote exploration and development of minerals and petroleum resources, in ever greater depths. Millions of barrels of oil and cubic feet of natural gas are pumped daily to the shore or offshore gathering platforms through pipelines. We should not discount the vulnerability of these offshore systems to sabotage or the environmental damage that an attack or accident might cause.

Petroleum shipped to the United States from overseas sources also presents a target for environmental terrorists. For waters under U.S. jurisdiction, the challenge will be to ensure the safety and seaworthiness of increasingly large ships, many of which will not be able to berth at U.S. ports because of draft limitations. This will drive the need for more offshore lightering, more offshore facilities, and the transshipment of hazardous materials through long and exposed pipelines. The prevention and response implications for the Coast Guard are obvious.

In addition, we must not underestimate the vulnerability of the maritime transport system to interruption, whether from natural or man-made disasters, piracy, or terrorist attack. The susceptibility of ships and key infrastructure elements is a problem that begs for a multifaceted solution.

. . . and Threats

The Department of Transportation's Strategic Plan 1997–2002 recognizes that "we must be prepared to face global markets, environmental challenges, transnational security threats, and a communications and information revolution." Secretary of Transportation Rodney Slater, warning of "terrorist threats, the increasing dependence on high technology transportation systems and communications networks, and increasing illegal immigrant transportation and smuggling," has underscored the need to scrutinize—and be able to counter—a broad range of threats to U.S. hemispheric maritime security. In this regard, the "Outcome Goals" identified by the Secretary will shape operational requirements for all Coast Guard assets:

Goal 1. Reduce vulnerability to and consequences of intentional harm to the transportation system and its users.

Goal 2. Ensure readiness and capability of all modes of commercial transportation to meet national security needs.

Goal 3. Ensure transportation, physical and information infrastructure, and technology are adequate to facilitate military logistics during mobility, training exercises, and mobilization.

Goal 4. Maintain readiness of resources, including operating forces and contingency resources owned, managed, or coordinated by the Department of Transportation necessary to support the President's National Security Strategy and other security-related plans.

Goal 5. Reduce flow of illegal drugs and illegal aliens.

The influx of illegal drugs is one of the nation's foremost national security problems. The Coast Guard is the lead maritime agency in the counterdrug effort, and despite the fact that interdiction occupies and consumes a tremendous amount of assets, this task is performed with little extra allocation. Drug interdiction remains difficult because it is assigned to multiple agencies; smugglers have high mobility; and there is a need for more vessels, aircraft, and personnel to patrol the vast U.S. coastlines and the six-million-square-mile Caribbean/eastern Pacific transit zone.

The Coast Guard has established Campaign Steel Web, a multiyear strategy aimed at reducing the supply of drugs to the United States. In 1997, Coast Guard cutters and aircraft deployed off South America and in the transit zone interdicted more than 103,600 pounds of cocaine, keeping more than 500 million "hits" off America's streets and out of our schools. The street value of the cocaine seized, estimated at $3.65 billion, exceeded the Coast Guard's entire 1997 operating budget by half a billion dollars. Still, this represents only an estimated 32% of the cocaine that entered the transit zone, pointing to the critical need for more effective intelligence, surveillance, and interdiction assets.

The influx of illegal drugs will become more difficult to counter as advanced equipment and technology increasingly are employed by drug cartels. In response to Coast Guard efforts, smugglers have begun investing in high-speed craft and low-observable/radar-evading vessels—even semisubmersibles—and aircraft in an attempt to avoid detection. Other capabilities include sophisticated counterinformation technologies that will enable criminals to challenge U.S. and world law enforcement organizations with greater boldness and daring.

Another of Secretary Slater's national security goals is to reduce the flow of illegal aliens entering the United States. For the Coast Guard, migrant interdiction operations are as much humanitarian efforts as they are law enforcement missions. Migrants typically take great risks and endure significant hardships in their attempts to flee their countries and enter the United States; their vessels often are overloaded and unseaworthy, lack basic safety equipment, and are operated by inexperienced mariners. The majority of alien migrant interdiction cases handled by the Coast Guard actually begin as search and rescue missions on the high seas.

Alien smuggling threatens the United States from all sides—along the East and West Coasts, in Hawaii, Guam, and Puerto Rico. Between 1980 and mid-1998, the Coast Guard interdicted 288,000 migrants from 43 countries. Economics and quality of life continue to be the primary factors driving people to brave the seas in the hope of reaching America. We have seen a marked increase in organized alien smuggling, especially from Cuba, the Dominican Republic, and the People's Republic of China.

In 1980, Coast Guard personnel stemmed a mass migration from Cuba, interdicting 125,000 illegal migrants who flooded toward Florida; U.S. Navy surface forces played key roles in supporting our afloat operations. In 1990–1991, Coast Guard deepwater assets responded to another mass migration, interdicting more than 37,600 Haitian migrants attempting to enter the United States illegally. In 1994, our cutters and aircraft responded to two nearly simultaneous mass migrations, working closely with Navy and other DoD assets. An afloat Coast Guard task force commander directed operations for the largest fleet of cutters since World War II, interdicting more than 25,300 Haitian migrants in Operation Able Manner and nearly 38,600 Cuban migrants in Operation Able Vigil.

The expected increase in the number of illegal migrants will create difficult social, economic, and political issues—including public discontent, strain on health care and social assistance systems of coastal states, and the overwhelming of detention facilities—which, in turn, will generate demands for effective Coast Guard interdiction operations farther out to sea. The need is great, therefore, for a cost-effective capability to interdict, and preferably deter, illegal migrant attempts.

These are just two of the threats to U.S. maritime security. Many others (see Table 1) are equally important and demand the same amount of attention. In response, the Coast Guard has envisioned a far-reaching program for the modernization and replacement of current cutter, aircraft, command-and-control, and shoreside infrastructure that will enable us to maintain a credible presence in key maritime regions to deter potential threats to U.S. sovereignty, to exercise sea control, and to project law enforcement action should deterrence fail.

Maritime Security Roles, Missions & Functions

The U.S. Coast Guard's roles and missions today touch on virtually every facet of the nation's maritime life. We are tasked with protecting U.S. citizens and interests in inland waterways, territorial seas, and exclusive

---

TABLE 1. MARITIME SECURITY CHALLENGES AND THREATS

- Smuggling of narcotics, illegal aliens, unauthorized technology transfers, and import of untaxed cargoes
- Growing complexities of multiflagged, multinational maritime/shipping corporations
- Violations of sanction restrictions placed by the United Nations or other international bodies
- Destabilizing arms trafficking
- Illegal transmission of key components or precursors for weapons of mass destruction
- Disruptions in maritime trade access
- Illegal exploitation or contamination of the market food supply
- Circumvention or violations of environmental protection laws
- Piracy, terrorism, and crime and violence at sea
- Sudden, uncontrolled mass migration
- Direct military threats to sealift support and port security needed to sustain military operations

Source: World Maritime Challenges, 1997. Office of Naval Intelligence.

economic zones under U.S. jurisdiction, as well as with detecting, deterring, and defeating threats to U.S. sovereignty that might arise on the high seas. The range of possible threats is likewise very broad, spanning economic, environmental, humanitarian, political, and military interests.

Throughout our history, however, the Coast Guard's core role has remained constant—to protect and defend U.S. citizens, interests, and friends, in waters under national jurisdiction as well as in overseas areas of importance to national security interests. This role, at its most fundamental level, has four elements:

- A humanitarian element dedicated to the preservation of lives and property at risk on the seas
- A policing element focused on national sovereignty and homeland defense, resource management, safety, and the maintenance of law and order at sea
- A diplomatic element in which Coast Guard people and platforms become instruments of U.S. foreign policy
- A military element in which Coast Guard assets link with other U.S. armed forces, as well as foreign militaries, in direct support of defense operations

We will continue to provide credible presence in and conduct surveillance of critical maritime regions; to detect, identify, and sort targets of interest; and to intercept and engage those targets. These core tasks must remain the basis for hemispheric maritime security throughout the 21st century, whether the mission is to rescue the distressed, to ensure safe maritime transport, to protect America's marine resources and environment, to uphold the law on the sea, or to safeguard U.S. diplomatic and military interests in regions around the world.

Deepwater Capabilities and Future

Unlike Coast Guard operations in coastal and inland waterways, deepwater missions typically call for a long term, continuous presence away from home stations. They require the ability to operate in severe environments—from Arctic to tropical climates—24 hours a day, every day, wherever the demands of national security require the Coast Guard's presence. The operational demands of our deepwater missions and tasks can be satisfied only with systems and platforms designed and engineered for this environment. That said, the adaptable and multimission character of deepwater cutter, aircraft, and command-and-control systems allows them to make significant contributions in virtually all operating areas. For example, deepwater cutters and command-control-and-communications system played key roles in the nation's responses to the *Exxon Valdez* (Prince William Sound, Alaska) and *Argo Merchant* (Nantucket, Massachusetts) oil spills in 1989 and 1976, as well as to the 1996 TWA Flight 800 disaster off Long Island.

The Coast Guard's existing deepwater systems that carry out current—let alone future—missions in support of hemispheric maritime security are reaching the end of their expected service lives. Performance increasingly is hampered, even as the threats we must counter are becoming more sophisticated and capable and the implications of poor Coast Guard mission performance grow more dire. The deepwater demands are compelling, calling for a multidimensional capability to carry out many diverse tasks simultaneously, across vast areas of ocean space (see Tables 2 and 3).

Recognizing the block obsolescence confronting much of the Coast Guard's deepwater force and the growing inability to meet our deepwater requirements effectively and efficiently, we have initiated the Integrated Deepwater Systems Capability Replacement Project, to upgrade,

TABLE 2. U.S. COAST GUARD DEEPWATER OPERATIONS

- 50 nautical miles or more from U.S. shores
- Long transit distance to operating areas
- Extended on-scene presence independent of support
- Sustained operations in severe weather/high seas
- Forward-deployed, often with other U.S. and allied/friendly forces

TABLE 3. DEEPWATER MISSIONS AND TASKS, 1998

- Search and rescue
- International ice patrol
- Humanitarian response
- General law enforcement
- Protection of living marine resources
- Maritime pollution enforcement and response
- Foreign vessel inspection
- Lightering zone enforcement
- Alien migrant, drug, and maritime interdiction
- Forward-deployed support to unified commanders
- Environmental defense
- U.S. homeland defense
- Port security and force protection
- Joint/combined combat operations

modernize, and replace aging ships, aircraft, and command-and-control infrastructure. This project is by far the largest acquisition project ever undertaken by the Coast Guard. Also, it is the first time that a federal agency has approached an acquisition program from an integrated, system-of-systems approach that embraces today's and tomorrow's sensors, command-and-control systems, shoreside facilities, boats and cutters, aircraft, and people in an innovative network-centric concept of operations.

A National Fleet for America

On 21 September 1998, Chief of Naval Operations Admiral Jay Johnson and I signed a joint Navy/Coast Guard policy statement on the National Fleet concept. In it, we commit to tailored operational integration of our multimission surface combatants and cutters, to reduce overlap and maximize our effectiveness across the range of naval and maritime missions. This partnership will allow us to coordinate surface ship planning, information systems integration, and research and development, as well as to expand joint concepts of operations, logistics, training, exercises, and deployments. As a result, we will be able to acquire and maintain future ships that both support and complement each service's roles and missions.

The benefits of such a coordinated and integrated approach already are apparent. They include meeting operational support and upgrade requirements more efficiently and economically; reduced acquisition costs; standardized training and cross-training in service-specific operational specialties; improved operational planning, integrated doctrinal and tactical development; much-enhanced force and unit interoperability; and, where it make sense, interoperability of technologies, systems, and platforms.

Admiral Johnson and I recognize the need to work together more effectively to ensure that the CNOs and commandants of 2010 and beyond have the means to accomplish the tasks at hand. Though much work lies ahead, I look forward to making this concept a reality.

The Course Ahead

The Coast Guard rarely has had to seek missions, especially in our deepwater operating area. Tasks have been mandated, usually in response to some specific national policy need and often without the allocation of additional resources. Fortunately, the Coast Guard has the spirit and discipline of a military service, combined with flexibility, readiness, and a commitment to civilian law enforcement, humanitarian service, and safety. This powerful blend has contributed to the Coast Guard's success during our first two centuries of service and is the tradition that will enable us to meet the demands of tomorrow.

14 "Coast Guard Missions: What We Do Now"

Jim Dolbow

(Selection from *The Coast Guardsman's Manual*, 10th Edition, Naval Institute Press, 2013): 23–29

EVERY DAY, THE COAST GUARD DEFENDS the nation, saves lives, leads humanitarian missions, protects the environment, and ensures the safety and security of the American people. On any given day, there is a Coast Guard high endurance cutter with an embarked helicopter patrolling the waters of the Bering Sea and enforcing fisheries law; a maritime safety and security team conducting ports, waterways, and coastal security missions in coastal waters of the Pacific; an HC-130 aircraft carrying out counter-drug operations in the Caribbean basin; icebreakers supporting the year-round flow of commercial goods on the Great Lakes and in the Northeast; and command centers monitoring vessel movements and mariner distress calls. Through this geographic diversity and broad set of competencies, combined with the Coast Guard's "bias for action," the Coast Guard is always ready as America's incident responder in the maritime domain.

These missions clearly demonstrate how the Coast Guard's assets, competencies, capabilities, authorities, and partnerships bring forth a unique ability to serve as a leading maritime responder and incident manager within government. By law, the Coast Guard has eleven statutory missions that are defined as either *homeland security* or *non-homeland security*.

Homeland Security Missions

Defense Readiness

As one of the nation's five armed services, the Coast Guard, via its Defense Operations program, provides unique authorities and capabilities to support the national military strategy. Specific objectives include defending the homeland, promoting international security, deterring conflict, and winning our nation's wars. The Coast Guard has the authorities, capabilities, and capacity to carry out homeland security and defense operations whether under Coast Guard control or under the control of combatant commanders. The Coast Guard maintains a level of readiness and training that allows for immediate integration with Department of Defense (DOD) forces for peacetime operations or during times of war. This supports U.S. national interests abroad, as well as facilitating DOD support to the Department of Homeland Security (DHS) for the integration of homeland defense and homeland security.

The major national defense missions assigned to the Coast Guard—maritime intercept operations, military environmental response, port operations, securities and defense, theater security operations, coastal sea control operations, rotary wing air intercept operations, combating terrorism operations, and maritime operational threat response support—are essential military tasks assigned to the Coast Guard as a component of joint and combined forces in peacetime, crisis, and war.

Moreover, outside of U.S. coastal waters, the Coast Guard assists foreign naval and maritime forces through training and joint operations. Many of the world's maritime nations have forces that operate principally in the littoral seas and conduct missions that resemble those of the Coast Guard. Since it has such a varied mix of assets and missions, the Coast Guard is a powerful role model that is in ever-increasing demand abroad. The service's close working relations with these nations not only improve mutual cooperation during specific joint operations in which the Coast Guard is involved but also support U.S. diplomatic efforts in general: promoting democracy, economic prosperity, and trust between nations.

Ports, Waterways, and Coastal Security (PWCS)

The PWCS mission entails the protection of the U.S. maritime domain and the U.S. Marine Transportation System (MTS) and those who live, work, or recreate near them; the prevention and disruption of terrorist attacks, sabotage, espionage, or subversive acts; and response to and recovery from those that do occur. Conducting PWCS deters terrorists from using or exploiting the MTS as a means for attacks on U.S. territory, population centers, vessels, critical infrastructure, and key resources. PWCS includes the employment of awareness activities; counterterrorism, antiterrorism, preparedness, and response operations; and the establishment and oversight of a maritime security regime. PWCS also includes the national defense role of protecting military outload operations.

Drug Interdiction

The Coast Guard is the lead federal agency for maritime drug interdiction and shares lead responsibility for air interdiction with the U.S. Customs Service. As such, it is a key player in combating the flow of illegal drugs to the United States. The Coast Guard's mission is to reduce the supply of drugs from the source by denying smugglers the use of air and maritime routes in the Transit Zone, a 6-million-square-mile area, including the Caribbean, Gulf of Mexico, and Eastern Pacific. In meeting the challenge of patrolling this vast area, the Coast Guard coordinates closely with other federal agencies and countries within the region to disrupt and deter the flow of illegal drugs.

Migrant Interdiction

The Coast Guard is the lead agency for the enforcement of U.S. immigration laws at sea. It conducts patrols and coordinates with other federal agencies and foreign countries to interdict undocumented migrants at sea, denying them entry via maritime routes to the United States, its territories, and possessions. Thousands of people try to enter this country illegally every year using maritime routes, many via smuggling operations. Interdicting migrants at sea means they can be quickly returned to their countries of origin without the costly processes required if they successfully enter the United States. Coast Guard migrant-interdiction operations in the Caribbean, the Gulf of Mexico, and the Eastern Pacific are as much humanitarian efforts as they are law-enforcement missions. In fact, the majority of migrant interdiction cases handled by the Coast Guard actually begin as search and rescue missions, usually on the high seas rather than in U.S. coastal waters.

Other Law Enforcement

Preventing illegal foreign fishing vessel encroachment in the Exclusive Economic Zone (EEZ) is a primary Coast Guard role vital to protecting the integrity of the nation's maritime borders and ensuring the health of U.S. fisheries. The Coast Guard also enforces international agreements to suppress damaging illegal, unreported, and unregulated (IUU) fishing activity on the high seas.

Non–Homeland Security Missions

Marine Safety

The Marine Safety program ensures the safe operation and navigation of U.S. and foreign-flagged vessels. The Coast Guard is responsible for providing safe, efficient, and environmentally sound waterways for commercial and recreational users. Domestic vessel inspections and port state control (foreign vessel) examinations are conducted in order to safeguard maritime commerce and international trade.

Search and Rescue

Search and Rescue (SAR) is one of the Coast Guard's oldest missions and perhaps the Coast Guard's best-known mission area. Minimizing the loss of life, injury, and property damage by rendering aid to persons and property in distress in the maritime environment has always been a Coast

Guard priority. Coast Guard SAR response involves multimission stations, cutters, aircraft, and boats linked by communications networks.

The National SAR Plan divides the U.S. area of SAR responsibility into internationally recognized inland and maritime SAR regions. The Coast Guard is the maritime SAR coordinator. To meet this responsibility, the Coast Guard maintains SAR facilities on the East, West, and Gulf coasts, in Alaska, Hawaii, Guam, and Puerto Rico, as well as on the Great Lakes and inland U.S. waterways. When the rescue alarm sounds, the Coast Guard is ready to confront the inherently dangerous maritime environment, frequently going into harm's way to save others. The Coast Guard works closely with other federal, state, and local agencies, and with foreign nations, to provide the world's fastest and most effective response to distress calls. It also maintains a vessel-tracking system called AMVER (automated mutual assistance vessel rescue) that allows it to divert nearby commercial vessels to render assistance when necessary.

Aids to Navigation and Waterways Management
The Aids to Navigation mission is a means for the Coast Guard to mark the waters of the United States and its territories to assist boaters in navigation and alert them to obstructions and hazards.

Living Marine Resources
This program's mission is to provide effective and professional at-sea enforcement of federal fisheries regulations and other regulations to advance national goals for the conservation and management of living marine resources and their environments through the detection and deterrence of illegal fishing activity. Beginning with the protection of the Bering Sea fur seal and sea otter herds and continuing through the vast expansion following World War II in the size and efficiency of global fishing fleets, Coast Guard responsibilities in this mission area now include enforcement of laws and treaties in the 3.36-million-square-mile U.S. Exclusive Economic Zone, the largest in the world.

Marine Environmental Protection

The Marine Environmental Protection program falls under the Coast Guard's stewardship role and is concerned with averting the introduction of invasive species, stopping unauthorized ocean dumping, and preventing the discharge of oil or hazardous substances into the navigable waters of the United States.

Ice Operations

This mission encompasses icebreaking activities in the Great Lakes, St. Lawrence Seaway, and Northeast. These activities facilitate the movement of bulk cargoes carried by regional commercial fleets during the winter months. In addition to domestic ice operations, the Coast Guard operates the only U.S.-controlled icebreakers capable of operations in the polar regions.

INDEX

SERIES EDITOR

THOMAS J. CUTLER has been serving the U.S. Navy in various capacities for more than fifty years. The author of many articles and books, including several editions of *The Bluejacket's Manual* and *A Sailor's History of the U.S. Navy,* he is currently the director of professional publishing at the Naval Institute Press and Fleet Professor of Strategy and Policy with the Naval War College. He has received the William P. Clements Award for Excellence in Education as military teacher of the year at the U.S. Naval Academy, the Alfred Thayer Mahan Award for Naval Literature, the U.S. Maritime Literature Award, the Naval Institute Press Author of the Year Award, and the Commodore Dudley Knox Lifetime Achievement Award in Naval History.

The Naval Institute Press is the book-publishing arm of the U.S. Naval Institute, a private, nonprofit, membership society for sea service professionals and others who share an interest in naval and maritime affairs. Established in 1873 at the U.S. Naval Academy in Annapolis, Maryland, where its offices remain today, the Naval Institute has members worldwide.

Members of the Naval Institute support the education programs of the society and receive the influential monthly magazine *Proceedings* or the colorful bimonthly magazine *Naval History* and discounts on fine nautical prints and on ship and aircraft photos. They also have access to the transcripts of the Institute's Oral History Program and get discounted admission to any of the Institute-sponsored seminars offered around the country.

The Naval Institute's book-publishing program, begun in 1898 with basic guides to naval practices, has broadened its scope to include books of more general interest. Now the Naval Institute Press publishes about seventy titles each year, ranging from how-to books on boating and navigation to battle histories, biographies, ship and aircraft guides, and novels. Institute members receive significant discounts on the Press' more than eight hundred books in print.

Full-time students are eligible for special half-price membership rates. Life memberships are also available.

For a free catalog describing Naval Institute Press books currently available, and for further information about joining the U.S. Naval Institute, please write to:

Member Services
U.S. NAVAL INSTITUTE
291 Wood Road
Annapolis, MD 21402-5034
Telephone: (800) 233-8764
Fax: (410) 571-1703
Web address: www.usni.org